# The reviews are in!
# THE BROADWAY DIARIES
# is a SMASH hit with readers.

"A celebration of Broadway from the perspective of its unsung heroes — the ushers and ticket takers. Pittman writes of his life in the theatre with style, grace, and humor, and his love for his work shines through in his writing."

— **ALLEN NEUNER**, *Out in Jersey*

"Pittman's tales of Broadway are told with warmth and love. A luscious peek behind the scenes and behind the man."

—**MICHAEL TAUSTINE**,
Head Treasurer, Lyceum Theatre

"To read anything by Joseph Pittman is to immediately take a trip to the most glorious days of Broadway history, to relive moments brought forth by a true insider who knows the secrets no one else does, and to wallow in precious memories of the greats as seen through his eyes. Whenever I've seen a post by Joseph in Broadway Remembered, I know I'm going to learn the best things I never knew about the stars I've always loved."

—**MICHAEL KAPE**, Founder, Broadway Remembered

"If you want to know EVERYTHING about EVERY Broadway production in the past 20-plus years —this is the book to read!!"

—**S. WALLIS**, former manager, Belasco Theatre

"Joseph Pittman's intricate detail and history of his time on Broadway really makes one know what it is like to work in a theatre. It shows how much working in the theatre can be a wonderful experience and can inspire others to do the same."

—**PAMELA LOETTERLE**, Sam S. Shubert Theatre usher

"I'm amazed at Pittman's breadth of knowledge and his storytelling prowess. It's like I'm on the aisle with him. Oh wait, I have been! A fun and insightful book about the history of Broadway."

—**DANNY BETANCOURT**, usher, The Broadway Theatre

"A witty, historical and hands-on account of 30 years of life in the theater. I could not put it down."

– **JOSEPH MARZULLO**, Veteran Broadway Photographer

"What an amazingly well-chronicled account of Joseph Pittman's 30 years on Broadway, working like a troubadour, taking on many parts and roles. This brings back many memories for me, as having worked in 'the office' for many years. I hope readers find this as fascinating as I did."

—**MARY BREILID**, Theatre Operations Director, The Shubert Organization, 1985-2019 (retired)

"Working on Broadway has been one of the greatest joys of my life. THE BROADWAY DIARIES is a perfect look inside what a thrill it is to work on the Great White Way. An insightful peek behind the scenes at a life spent in the house, you will be captivated by every song and dance Pittman has to show you."

—**SARAH W. WAXMAN**, Merchandise Manager, Covid Safety Manager

"During the nearly two years that the COVID pandemic shutdown all Broadway Theatres, the prolific fiction writer Joseph Pittman produced a personal blog. Part daily musing, part memoir, part tales from a Broadway insider and part story of a working-class hero, that blog has now led to THE BROADWAY DIARIES. These stories will delight any fan of Broadway Theatre and the untold story of the theatre world. Mr. Pittman shares the inside skinny on the life inside Broadway theatres, on the "House" side of the curtain. Pittman's love of the theatre is visceral as he tells the story of his arrival from the hinterlands of upstate New York, how he found his way into the world of Broadway and rises through the ranks of the unsung and usually anonymous Front of House Broadway theatre staff. Mr. Pitman's sense of humor is front and center as he regales us with the comings and goings of the luminaries who without their realizing it cross his path and are observed by his sharp eye. This is a joyous read, like taking a trip with an old friend."

—**TOM STEIN**, Manager, Theatre Facilities, The Shubert Organization (retired)

# THE BROADWAY DIARIES
## 30 Years from Aisle to Stage

**EVER WONDER** about the person who just handed you a Playbill? Of course not.

Ushers, ticket takers, those who work the front of the house on Broadway are often the unsung workers of the Great White Way. But in this heartfelt, funny, informative memoir of Broadway's past, readers will get to know what it really takes to raise that curtain.

The stories here will answer such burning questions as:

What made Kathleen Turner nearly stop the show during a performance of *The Graduate*?

What night was *Taboo* sold out?

What star misspelled an iconic word while on stage at *The 25th Annual Putnam County Spelling Bee*?

Are there ghosts on Broadway, and where — and who — do they haunt?

What's the oldest still-operating theatre on Broadway, and what was its first show?

Name your favorite modern-day Mama Rose? Tyne, Bernadette, Patti?

How many theatres has the revival of *Chicago* played? It's a trick question.

Who was your favorite Broadway Hedwig?

**THE BROADWAY DIARIES** is a glimpse at a Broadway rarely seen, the shared experience of a group of people from all walks of life who come to their aisles, ready to seat the patrons, sometimes just for a Wednesday matinee, often working an entire run of the show, or staying on for years. Forget the critics, if you want to know how audiences really feel about a play or musical? Ask the usher.

They'll also tell you where the restrooms are.

*Also by Joseph Pittman*

**The Linden Corners Novels:**
TILTING AT WINDMILLS
A CHRISTMAS WISH
A CHRISTMAS HOPE
A CHRISTMAS DREAM
(Originally published as THE MEMORY TREE)
CHASING WINDMILLS

**The Todd Gleason Crime Series:**
LONDON FROG
CALIFORNIA SCHEMING
TWO TODD TALES
TWO MORE TODD TALES
THE CANNES CON

**Stand Alone Novels:**
WHEN THE WORLD WAS SMALL
LEGEND'S END
BEYOND THE STORM

**The Eckert's Landing Trilogy:**
THE ORIGINAL CRIME: Remembrance
THE ORIGINAL CRIME: Retribution
THE ORGINAL CRIME: Redemption

THE SHADOW DIARIES:
The Hopeful Year in the Life of a Rescue Dog

# THE BROADWAY DIARIES

## 30 YEARS FROM AISLE TO STAGE

Joseph Pittman

LINDEN CORNERS PRESS

THE BROADWAY DIARIES

Copyright © 2022 by Joseph Pittman
All rights reserved, including the right of reproduction in whole or in part in any form.

Published by Linden Corners Press
Keyport, NJ 07735
www.lindencornerspress.com
ISBN: 978-1-7379082-1-0 (eBook)
978-1-7379082-2-7 (print)

Cover Design: Steven Cummings
Interior and Back Cover Design by Victor Mingovits

Tony Award® is an acknowledged copyright of the American Theatre Wing and The Broadway League. www.tonysawards.com

Playbill® is an acknowledged copyright of Playbill Incorporated. www.playbill.com

None of the theatre chains referenced in this work were involved in, nor have corporately endorsed, the development of this memoir. The Shubert Organization, The Nederlander Organization, Jujamcyn Theatres, and Circle in the Square remain independent of these recollections, which are solely owned by the author.

This book is licensed to the original purchaser only. Duplication or distribution via any means is illegal and a violation of International Copyright Law, subject to criminal prosecution and upon conviction, fines and/or imprisonment. The eBook edition cannot be legally loaned or given to others. No part of this book can be shared or reproduced without the express permission of the publisher.

*This one's for...*
*Anyone who has ever attended a Broadway show.*
*We can't do this without you.*

**INTRODUCTION:** Broadway Salutes..........................xvii

**ACT ONE:** The House is Open..............................1

**DIARY ONE:** To the Balcony..................................3
**DIARY TWO:** Local B-183......................................7
**DIARY THREE:** Everything's Coming up Joseph.........11
**DIARY FOUR:** A Summer of No-Necked Monsters......15
**DIARY FIVE:** The Mask Ahead of Its Time................19
**DIARY SIX:** Yes, Virginia, there is a Tony Award.......23
**DIARY SEVEN:** The Independents, Part 1.................27
**DIARY EIGHT:** The Independents, Part 2.................33
**DIARY NINE:** The Boys from Syracuse ....................39
**DIARY TEN:** Disorder in the Cort...........................45
**DIARY ELEVEN:** Ghostly Memories .......................49
**DIARY TWELVE:** A Night with the Lyceum...............55
**DIARY THIRTEEN:** The Tony that Got Away .............59
**DIARY FOURTEEN:** Waiting for the Fat Lady to Sing....65
**DIARY FIFTEEN:** Indiscreet Sisters, Husbands,
   and Sushi......................................................71
**DIARY SIXTEEN:** Anarchy in the Aisles...................77
**DIARY SEVENTEEN:** Don't Change My Name,
   I'm Good Luck................................................81

DIARY EIGHTEEN: We Live on Avenue B .................87
DIARY NINETEEN: Broadway 2021........................93
DIARY TWENTY: I Give My Regards, Sir Harrison ......97
DIARY TWENTY-ONE: The Royale Family................ 103
DIARY TWENTY-TWO: Four Tonys and a Funeral....... 107
DIARY TWENTY-THREE: The Litter Box ................. 113
DIARY TWENTY-FOUR: In this Corner…Fernando ..... 117
DIARY TWENTY-FIVE: The Great Hair-Flip of 1997.... 123
DIARY TWENTY-SIX: At Least There was No Math .... 129

INTERMISSION: Remembering Sondheim............. 135

ACT TWO: Please Take Your Seats...................... 139

DIARY TWENTY-SEVEN: One of the Great Ones......... 141
DIARY TWENTY-EIGHT: Drink with Me................... 147
DIARY TWENTY-NINE: I Put on Some Make-up......... 153
DIARY THIRTY: Turn Up the 8-Track ................... 159
DIARY THIRTY-ONE: And Pull a Wig Down
    from the Shelf......................................... 165
DIARY THIRTY-TWO: Is it Mourning Yet?................ 171
DIARY THIRTY-THREE: To Kong, With Love............. 177
DIARY THIRTY-FOUR: The Berlin Secret................. 185
DIARY THIRTY-FIVE: Let There Be Peace on Earth .... 191
DIARY THIRTY-SIX: Circle X 3…and More ............... 197
DIARY THIRTY-SEVEN: I'd Like to
    Thank the Tony People ............................. 203
DIARY THIRTY-EIGHT: Canceled Culture................ 209

**DIARY THIRTY-NINE:** Um,
   It's JOHN Wilkes Booth........................... 215
**DIARY FORTY:** A Strange Show Just
   Passing Through....................................... 221
**DIARY FORTY-ONE:** The Balcony is Closed.............. 227
**DIARY FORTY-TWO:** A Reopening While
   on the Verge of Tears................................. 233
**DIARY FORTY-THREE:** I'll Have What He's Having..... 239
**DIARY FORTY-FOUR:** War, Told in Pieces................ 245
**DIARY FORTY-FIVE:** You'd Like to Win a Tony?......... 251
**DIARY FORTY-SIX:** I've Seen Kathleen Turner
   Naked and She Has No Idea Who I Am .......... 257
**DIARY FORTY-SEVEN:** Broadway
   Dreams and Nightmares .......................... 263
**DIARY FORTY-EIGHT:** Are You Ready for
   Some Football?......................................... 269
**DIARY FORTY-NINE:** Jesus Takes the Circle............ 275
**DIARY FIFTY:** Another Opening, Another Closing..... 281
**DIARY FIFTY-ONE:** Mulled Wine for Everyone! ........ 289
**DIARY FIFTY-TWO:** The 11 O'clock Number............. 295

**ENCORE:** The Bishop of Broadway Strikes Again..... 301

## INTRODUCTION

# Broadway Salutes

This memoir is all my dog's fault.

Shadow is a beautiful and sweet-natured Black Lab/Greyhound mix, who entered our lives on December 28$^{th}$, 2018. So cute, so funny, so…expressive and quirky. As a writer, I could see the words in those soulful amber eyes of his itching to come out. As a rescue, he had his story to tell about his first year living with his two new daddies. I know the feeling. I like telling stories, too.

I wrote a year-long Facebook blog called THE SHADOW DIARIES, and the next year, suddenly, hey, it was a published book. With a beautiful cover done by none other than Shadow's other daddy, an accomplished artist and teacher, Steve, the book was a true family affair.

I got to thinking…what could I write next? I did another full year's worth of diary entries centered on the writing process and the publication of my books, both under my name and that of my pseudonym, Adam Carpenter—44 books and counting to date. Perhaps I'll one-day publish that manuscript. But it was written more for me, to preserve memories secured in my mind.

That was 2020, and it gave me hope during as we all know a difficult time in our world hit us. I write fiction, primarily, so my created worlds of Todd Gleason and Jimmy McSwain offered up a great escape during that year. Todd stars in my funny crime novels, while Jimmy McSwain's noir life imbues the New York I love. Indulging these characters and their stories got me through the early months of the pandemic.

And then came 2021, and there seemed no end in sight. Where was my theatre life?

When you're living on your sofa and your job is on hold because the world is shutdown, it's only natural that your mind drifts toward a new project—at least, that's what my mind does. Thus I began what was dubbed, of course, THE BROADWAY DIARIES, a natural follow-up to both THE SHADOW DIARIES and THE WRITER DIARIES. Again, I offered up a weekly FB post, this time sharing my experiences working as a front of the house employee on Broadway, mostly as an usher but also in the role of ticket taker. Same union, just different job responsibilities.

The end result of telling those stories is this book, a look back at not just my own memories of working on Broadway, but of the shows I worked, the actors I encountered, and the theatres that housed them. I hopefully enriched my stories with the history of Broadway, but primarily centered on the time period from April 8, 1990 to March 12, 2020, the years I worked for these theatres, 8-shows a week for 30 years, with few breaks in between shows closing and theatres reopening.

But the idea for a theatrical memoir actually began to take shape in 2015. **HEDWIG AND THE ANGRY INCH** had just closed its critical and commercial success at the Belasco Theatre, and I was taking a couple weeks of vacation, visiting family in upstate New York. Then came two fortuitous moments—a phone call from the head usher at the Golden Theatre to work the upcoming week as an usher; a new show was opening. I wasn't sure I wanted to return to the city just yet, but then she called me back and said she needed me on the door as ticket taker. I like that job more! I jumped on Amtrak the next day to be back in time for the 8:00 pm first preview of **THE GIN GAME** starring Cicely Tyson and James Earl Jones.

The second moment was also taking place that day. Since I'd been away, I hadn't seen my mail, but through the magic of Facebook I learned that the ceremony of "Broadway Salutes" was taking place that afternoon. It's an annual event where the combined forces of The Broadway League and the Coalition of Broadway Unions and Guilds honor those individuals who are celebrating a milestone year—for me, it was 25 years. The date was Tuesday, September 29, 2015. The invitation had been sitting in my mailbox.

I was fortunately able to make the ceremony, dressed in my ticket taker suit, sitting outside on West 43$^{rd}$

Street in the warm heat of an Indian Summer. I saw my name on a giant billboard in Times Square (along with all the other inductees), had my name called and was then invited up to the dais where I was pinned with my 25-Year lapel pin. I even had my photograph taken and it was posted on Broadway.com.

That's just one of my Broadway memories, but what that day did was help solidify my sense of accomplishment in a world where art meets passion, where passion meets commitment, where commitment meets devotion. What follows in these pages is 30 years of stories and of shows and of theatres, and of a life found *before* the wicked stage. I hope you'll enjoy this trip down the streets of the Great White Way as much as I enjoyed reliving them.

*—Joseph Pittman, February 2022*

# ACT ONE
## The House is Open

## DIARY ONE

# To the Balcony

Let's begin with a simple question: do you remember your first Broadway show?

In this introductory diary entry, I'm going to detail how I became interested in theatre. It begins back when I was a teenager, getting bit by the theater bug.

At Eagle-Hill Middle School, I was a member of the Chorale, and it was there where I first started to sing show tunes. In addition, I was taking piano lessons, and among the sheets of music my teacher provided was the score for **FIDDLER ON THE ROOF**. In truth, I didn't think I had the talent to pursue playing an instrument, and so after two years I stopped.

But I kept singing. Fayetteville-Manlius High School, I was in the regular choir class, but then I also tried out for the Chorale, and made it. I remember my voice hadn't exactly changed yet, so I stood at the edge of the tenor section, right next to the altos. I was told to sing whichever part my voice could handle. We sang from **PIPPIN** and **A CHORUS LINE** and **FAME**.

As I continued to sing, I ended up taking a course the second half of my sophomore year. We had a choice: speech class, or something called Theater Games. The latter sounded more fun, and so I signed up. It was a lot of improv, and I got to play with voices and different characters of varying ages. That class helped me come out of my shell. Life upon the stage has a tendency to do that because you can be other people.

At the end of the school year, the teacher, who was also the drama director, told me he expected me to try out for the school productions the next year. Each school year F-M would do a play in the fall and a musical in the spring. My junior year, the play was **OUR TOWN**. I would play the role of Joe Crowell, the paperboy (which I was in real-life). In the spring, we did the Rodgers & Hart classic, **BABES IN ARMS**. A great show and score, and I was happy to be a part of it. I was put in the chorus ensemble.

Okay, senior year, the play was Bel Kaufman's **UP THE DOWN STAIRCASE**. I was cast in the minor speaking role of Lenny, the class clown. Boy, did I milk it for all it was worth! The musical was **SOUTH PACIFIC** that spring, and being assigned, in act one, as one of the seebees. Act II I had a speaking part, that of Lt. Buzz Adams, the pilot who flies Emile and Cable during Operation: Alligator. I liked my costume, a navy hat with silver bars, and a leather jacket. I still have that hat.

The other big event that final year of high school was landing a spot in a group called Swing Sixteen. Eight boys, eight girls, four from each vocal range. We actually traveled the state, performed at colleges and other high schools, and even took a road trip to New Jersey, where we all stayed with local families. I remember we were doing "The Telephone Song" from **BYE BYE, BIRDIE**, and I was asked to play the role of the nerdy kid, Harvey Johnson, who kept calling if "Charity was home from school yet." It was fun, except for one night when I missed my entry cue.

Ok, back to my earlier question. Do you remember the first show you saw in a Broadway theatre?

I do, while going on our senior trip to New York City in April of 1982, our class attended, of course, **A CHORUS LINE**. At the Shubert Theatre on 44th Street. It was a Thursday night, and our seats were way high up in the balcony. I would later work that balcony as an usher, and when there I'd imagine that 17-year-old kid who suffered from a bit of vertigo.

That Saturday, we attended our second show, **EVITA**, at the Broadway Theatre, our seats far up in the Rear Mezzanine of this cavernous theatre. It was a matinee, a word I would later have a love/hate relationship with. I would end up years later working at the Broadway, but more on that theatre as we take our tour up and down of these streets of theatrical dreams.

I hope you'll all follow me along throughout this book as I write about my corner of the sky. I've got magic to do, just for you.

DIARY TWO

# Local B-183

This is an origins story. Just how did I become a Broadway usher, and more importantly, why, and in the end, what made me stick with it for so long? Ah, I love how it began and why I stuck with it. As for the why? Well, it was initially financial.

It's 1990. Yeah, I was a young-ish lad living in New York City. My main pursuit was publishing, and later, writing, but life had a way of twisting your destiny. As a 24-year-old editorial assistant working for Bantam Books and having just secured my first (and as it turned out, only) Manhattan apartment, truth be told: I needed some more cash to pay for it.

The way I ended up working on Broadway is a three-tiered story.

I've already detailed my first-ever show. So, let's shift forward and start with the first show I saw after I had moved to NYC. It was the original production of **LES MISERABLES** at the Broadway Theatre. We had good seats, Orchestra Row O, on the aisle. Wait, who is this "we" I speak of? It was a birthday present from my then-girlfriend (ok, I'll wait for the laughter to subside), Katherine. She knew I liked the score and so she treated me to tickets. She broke up with me five days later. Guess I liked the show too much.

Okay, second part, a year later. Broadway tickets were kind of beyond the price range for someone working an entry level publishing position, but with a visit to TKTS (the discount day-of-performance ticket center in Times Square), my co-worker and friend Charlene secured tickets for that night's performance of **CATS**. If I have one memory of that night, it's that I was seated by a young, male usher.

Guess that made an impression on me.

Third part of the story, and this is where my idea took hold. Since I worked during the day, 9-5, what about a night/weekend job? I started my due diligence, walking around the theater district, asking about becoming an usher. I stopped at box offices, mostly, asking to speak with the manager. Nope, I got nowhere. Then, after having exhausted myself through six or seven theatres and facing the proverbial slammed door, I encountered an employee outside the St. James Theatre. I asked her about ushering.

"It's a union. You gotta join."

I asked for any information she could provide. It was then called the Local B-183, and I was generously given the phone number. Feeling confident, I called the next week; it was a Thursday afternoon around 3:00.

"Hi, I'm interested in ushering," I said to the gruff-voiced lady on the other end. She quickly informed me they weren't hiring and hung up on me, again, quickly. That was not a promising beginning.

But for anyone who knows me, I have a stubborn streak. I persevere when I want something, no is something I like to turn into a yes. And this was something I wanted. I waited exactly a week, called that next Thursday, same time. Same lady, same gruff greeting. I asked about ushering.

There was a pause. Then, "Can you work tonight?"

It was three o'clock in the afternoon. I was still at my day job, and I was ill-prepared for such a sudden request. My answer of course was: "yes." And that simple word changed the entire trajectory of my life. I was instructed to show up at 7:00 pm, black pants, white shirt, black tie, at the Marquis Theatre. "Ask for Lulu, tell her Bobsy sent you."

I loved them already by their names alone. Okay, maybe Bobsy's voice, too.

I showed up and was told I would be training that night. I wouldn't get paid, just learn the ropes by trailing another usher. Um, ok. At least I was there—on Broadway. Five minutes before the house opened, Lulu informed me they were short an usher. Which meant they needed me to fill in and work an aisle. I was told I'd get paid; I was "on" till the end of the show (more on our lingo in a future diary). But it was the last thing she said that made me smile.

"Oh, and can you work the rest of the week?"

I got a Friday night, two on Saturday, and two Sunday shows (the last of which were paid at time-and-a-half). I was in! The usher Fran who worked the aisle near me helped me out, gave me the greatest piece of advice I've ever received about doing this job: always know your fifth seat in. I'll explain as we go along.

So, there I was working Broadway, but not exactly seeing the ideal show. **OBA OBA '90**: The Hit Brazilian Musical Revue. Not my first choice, but hey, I got paid for seven shows that week! I could buy groceries!

This was just the start of 30 years of shows and experiences. The point was: I was part of an exclusive world so few knew about or understood. Ushers are anonymous to the patrons, an exchange like a passing breeze. But not with each other. The things I would learn along the way about who worked what aisle, how, and why. The drama would not be just kept to the stage!

DIARY THREE

# Everything's Coming up Joseph

My transition from having just a day job to always working coincided with my securing an apartment in Manhattan. When I first started ushering, I was in Queens, Kew Gardens specifically. But I was on the hunt for a place on the Upper East Side. I finally got it, and as thrilled as I was, an early conflict arose. I'd been asked to work at the theatre on moving day.

I wrote about **OBA OBA '90**, but to stay active in this new world of mine, well…you gotta call and let them know you want to work anywhere and everywhere. I called the union office, and back then, most of the houses they filled were what were known then as "the independents." That meant the Nederlander- and Jujamcyn-owned theatres. The union rarely gave out usher work for the Shubert Organization.

Ah, Shubert work, it evaded me in the early days. I once called their office after I'd done my first few shifts and the longtime employee who gave out usher work said, again, in a gruff smoker's voice, "I don't know you,

I got nothing for you." I never called her again. But, that week the union had a Shubert house on offer to me, a Saturday matinee.

It was at the Ambassador, a play called **THE CIRCLE**, starring Rex Harrison (in his final Broadway role). I was excited to land the gig, but the problem was I had to be dressed and ready by 1:00 pm that Saturday. But it coincided with…moving and unpacking and bringing all my stuff up three flights of stairs. No elevator.

I'd rented a U-Haul, readied my belongings, my books and furniture, all set to fulfill my dream of living on Manhattan's UES. Wasn't that where the rich people lived? (Alas, not those who resided near $2^{nd}$ Ave.). I had two friends helping that day, and sure, we got an early start, but I knew I'd never be able to make that call time.

What's a new usher who is trying to prove himself reliable to his new employer to do? I called that Friday, the day before, and explained why I had to turn down the work. The one and only time I ever said "No" to a shift. But they were understanding, responding by saying, "Will you be done moving in time for an evening shift?"

Don't say no twice. I accepted it, and with boxes strewn all over my apartment at 311, with the U-Haul safely returned, I had little time to get myself to the St. James Theatre for a 7:00 p.m. arrival. Oh, and the best part? Yeah, while I'd given away the Saturday matinee at the Ambassador, I got not only the Saturday night show, but this request: "Can you work the Sunday matinee, too?"

The show was **GYPSY**, starring Tyne Daly. I'll confess I wasn't a big fan of hers. "Cagney & Lacey" just wasn't my thing. But...wow. Did that woman own that stage, that show, that theatre and that block. Baby June might get to sing "Let Me Entertain You," but Tyne was the one doing the entertaining. Working way up in the balcony (ten rows, so steep), I'd never seen anything like it. Her "Rose's Turn" was more like "Tyne's Turn."

The chief at the St. James offered me a few more shows the next week, and then the next. I would just sit there on the steps (I even got offered to work the mezzanine, which was an upgrade over that steep balcony, ironically a downgrade by level) and watch the magic every night. That production of **GYPSY** remains to this day one of my favorites. I'll tell my Tyne encounter in a future diary.

But life in the theatre is transient, and you move from theatre to theatre. You call the office; you get a show or two. You make that extra money that helps you pay the Manhattan rent. But what you are seeking is an experience, an artform at its best, talent on the stage and behind the scenes, a slice of the world you realize is a gift.

Little lambs, my **GYPSY** days were over. But I was fully ensconced at 311, an editorial assistant by day, an usher by night (and by weekend), living a life of books and live theatre, always dreaming of being a published author. That would have to wait. Because the daily question was where next would I be seating people?

There's a unique theatre on Broadway called Circle in the Square. Only 700 or so seats, depending upon the staging requirements of a specific production. It could be configured in a true square or rectangle, a horseshoe-shape, whatever the director and designer wanted. I was sent there for a Saturday matinee after my St. James run had ended. A play called **ZOYA'S APARTMENT**, starring Bronson Pinchot. (Yeah, Balki from "Perfect Strangers"). The seating plan was so strange, different from other theatres and I had to learn it fast.

It would be ten years before I'd work Circle again, and it proved life-changing for many reasons. I ended up having a rich history with that theatre. More on those stories later. Until then, there are many more theatres to explore.

DIARY FOUR

# A Summer of No-Necked Monsters

Let me tell you about the first summer I spent with Kathleen Turner. So many nights and a few matinees, and oh, how she looked in that alluring slip of hers, her cascading hair, as she made her entrance at the top of the show. And that opening line, that Southern drawl mixed with her smoky voice: "Brick, one of those no-necked monsters hit me with a hot-buttered biscuit so I have to change," I can still hear it.

I'm talking about **CAT ON A HOT TIN ROOF**, the classic drama by Tennessee Williams, playing a limited run at the Eugene O'Neill Theatre on 49th Street. The union called my home number and left a message on my answering machine with the assignment; I got the message just in time—and yes, pre-cell phone. That was one day in May of 1990, and I didn't work another theatre until the show closed in August.

Here's what happened. The staff seemed to like me, or more specifically the head usher did (sometimes called a chief usher). Helen ran a great house, and I liked being her "regular" substitute usher for when one of her permanents had to take off. I didn't know a chief could give out work without going through the union first, but she did, and I averaged about six shows a week.

I loved the trust she put in this newbie and I never turned down a shift. But all those shifts made for some long nights. I was of course still working my publishing job M-F, 9-5 or so, and then pulling down those shows at night and all weekend. **CAT** was nearly 3-hours in length, three acts, two intermissions. And always sold out.

Ms. Turner was a big movie star and the poster for the show was a drawing card. But there were other names in the starry production. I knew of Daniel Hugh-Kelly from a TV show called "Hardcastle & McCormick," ("Ryan's Hope" anyone?) and then there was Charles Durning (he won the Tony for playing Big Daddy), and Polly Holliday, who I knew as Flo from "Alice." A character actor who played Chester on "Newhart" always made me laugh, and a then-unknown actress named Debra Jo Rupp played the mother of those no-necked monsters.

Ms. Rupp would later guest in memorable roles on "Seinfeld," "Friends," and star on "That 70's Show." Perfect comic timing.

When you work as a sub usher (and you're new to the business), you take what's offered and you put in your time, your hours. With six shifts a week, I would usually be "on" for five of them. Helen would give me an "off," usually on a double-show Saturday. On meant you stayed till the end. Off meant you got to leave 20 minutes into the show.

How many nights did I sit on the stairs of the mezzanine, watching the drama unfold? The sound engineer, who sat nearby, was like, "why are you always on late?" Because that's how it worked. I kept getting asked back and I was enjoying the paycheck. And the show. To hear that poetic language, delivered with precision by such a great cast, there was nothing to complain about. (Except when I'd get home at midnight and my alarm would go off at 7:00 a.m.)

There were many benefits to working the same show. First of all, I knew my schedule in advance, so I didn't have to call the office, wondering which theatre I was going to be sent to. And I didn't have to constantly be carrying my uniform, since the O'Neill let me use a locker in the usher's room. I also got to know Manhattan better. I'd only been living at 311 for about a month, and as the season grew warmer outside, I would often walk to the theatre on weekends. From $90^{th}$ and $2^{nd}$ to $49^{th}$ and $8^{th}$. I usually walked through Central Park.

But not before I'd stopped at the Green Farm Deli on Madison Avenue, bought a blueberry muffin and a Diet Coke. (That's how I actually survived a 3-hour show!)

I was sorry when the show reached its announced closing date, wondering where or even if I'd end up at another theatre. The O'Neill hadn't yet booked a new show, so I had to go find a new theatre. By being the intrepid self that I was when first considering this job, I sought out work beyond what the union could do for me. And I'd find work the week after closing —that's its own diary entry.

**CAT ON A HOT TIN ROOF** wouldn't be my last theatrical experience with Ms. Turner. I would work two more runs of shows that she starred in, but again, that's for another time or two as well. I did once escort her down to a seat at a show when I was ushering at the Belasco, and I mentioned that I'd worked so many of her Broadway shows.

"Dahling, aren't you sweet." There she was, not being seen from the mezzanine but on my arm, that sultry voice of hers sparking memories of no-necked monsters. She was Maggie the Cat once more.

DIARY FIVE

# The Mask Ahead of its Time

So far, I've been going chronologically with my memories of working on Broadway. But this one is going to be more themed-oriented. A single show, a single theatre, because ever since I've been working on Broadway, this theatre has housed only one show.

When I moved back to New York City (I'd been born in Queens, but the family moved upstate when I was seven-years-old), **THE PHANTOM OF THE OPERA** was the hottest show in town. You couldn't get a ticket, and if you could it cost more than my rent (at 1988 ticket prices). I had bought the cast album already, and along with **LES MISERABLES**, I listened to it a lot. By the first time I saw it, I knew the score well. But to see it live…wow.

Even though I was by now working as an usher, I hadn't yet cracked the Shubert code. I was still working "the independents." So, my co-worker and friend Linda and I bought tickets for **PHANTOM**, with seats in Row F of the Rear Mezzanine. A section I would end up working so many times. A patron would come in and have a ticket for 106 and I would think: hey, that's my seat!

But that night, as the chandelier rose during the overture to the heights of the Majestic (an aptly named theatre), I was enthralled. The three original leads had departed the show by that point. But as luck would have it, I got to hear the most gorgeous, soaring soprano voice I'd ever heard. An actress/singer by the name of Rebecca Luker. Truly an angel of music.

A year later, a new Mary had been installed in the job of handing out the work at Shubert, and I placed a call and with the stars in alignment I was hired, I was in. Broadening my Broadway connections. Though the first show I was sent to was **MISS SAIGON**, again a last-minute Thursday night gig up at the Broadway Theatre, after that for the following three weeks I was sent, eight shows a week, to the Majestic. **PHANTOM** was haunting me.

I made some great new friends during my weeks there and continue to through the connections available on social media. Some of us would go out for drinks after a Friday or Saturday night performance. Over the years, I would work **PHANTOM** so many times I could hum the exit music note by note. I even got to attend the show's yearly anniversary parties to celebrate their milestones on Broadway. I think I went to the 5$^{th}$, 10$^{th}$, and 15$^{th}$.

I also remember a time when my parents were coming to New York for a visit, and they wanted to see a show (they actually saw two that Saturday). With help from the Shubert main office, I was able to secure "house seats" (yes, you have to pay for them) for my parents. But the seats were awesome. Second row, center orchestra. I remember watching from the mezzanine level as the chandelier, at the end of Act One, swooped over their heads.

The Majestic is the second largest of the 17 Shubert-owned theatres, with a capacity of 1645 seats. Whenever I worked there, I was usually assigned to usher in the mezzanine. Once the house opened and the audience started coming up those stairs, you kind of had to take a deep breath and then go into usher mode. A lot of people to get seated in 30 minutes time, plus seating late-comers in the dark, your flashlight and instinct as your guides.

But there was one night when I finally made it down to center orchestra—and yes, what aisle you work is a status sign in our world. It was December 31st, sometime in the 90s, back when Broadway could still have New Year's Eve performances and it was considered a big event. Lots of regular ushers would take off, so I offered up my services. The show would be over by 10:30. I could still ring in the New Year with friends.

That night, I was assigned to the same section where my parents had sat, and I had to remain on the orchestra level during the performance. I'd never seen the show like this, so close. I was mesmerized all over again, and over the years whenever I would sub at the Majestic so many of these memories would come to me. I always recommend the show to anyone who hasn't seen a Broadway show.

More recently, **PHANTOM** changed their performance schedule, instituting a rare (for Broadway) Thursday matinee. By then I had been moved up to the title of Ticket taker, and the Majestic needed someone to fill in on those afternoons. The Majestic being a large house, there were two ticket takers, and for a couple of months I had a great time working with my pal Perry. Being on the front door made me realize I'd come a long way from taking late-comers up to Row L in the rear mezzanine.

I always had a connection with **PHANTOM**. In 2010, my father passed away of the horrible disease known as ALS. In 2020, Ms. Luker passed away of the same disease. Two voices silenced, but memories stirred, an unlikely connection and a parallel during this trying time. There's a song in Act 2: "Wishing You Were Somehow Here Again."

January 26, 2021 was Phantom's 33$^{rd}$ birthday, still silenced by the pandemic. But, despite what the Phantom sings at the end of the show —"It's over now, the music of the night" —we all know that's not true. **THE PHANTOM OF THE OPERA** *is* Broadway.

## DIARY SIX

# Yes, Virginia, there is a Tony Award

Night has come, I'm thinking about the devils that lurk in the shadows, making their move against the unsuspecting and the innocent. But then there are the angels around us, living in a city of three million people...but wait, easily half of them up to no good. A city of angels... try and find one.

That's what the window card stated. Yup, **CITY OF ANGELS**, still one of my most favorite shows, at a theatre filled with memories, and an experience which helped further shape my life as a wannabe and eventual mystery writer. I spent over a year working the Tony-winning show, the then-named Virginia Theatre like a second home.

**CITY OF ANGELS** is set in the Los Angeles of the 1940s. It features a writer—and his detective—in concurrent stories. One done in black and white. The other in color. Still one of the best directed shows (by Michael Blakemore) I've ever seen. Stine wrote the book; Stone solved crimes. But life in Hollywood means you turn everything into a movie, and when it comes to detective fiction…trust no one. Especially the studio executive.

Music by Cy Coleman (my favorite Broadway composer), smart lyrics by David Zippel, and a brilliant, witty book by Larry Gelbart, for this young kid seating people and then sitting on the stairs of the theatre every chance he got, well, he knew he was watching something special unfold. "She had the kind of face a man could hang a dream on, a body that made the Venus de Milo look all thumbs, and only the floor kept her legs from going on forever."

I was hooked from that opening voiceover. It established tone, character, humor, noir, and the show only kept at its twists and turns until the final "Hollywood ending." I was still new to this ushering world, so I wasn't familiar with many Broadway actors. Greg Edelman, James Naughton, Randy Graff, Rachel York, Dee Hoty. The only familiar name was Rene Auberjunois, who I knew from the sitcom "Benson."

Here's how I happened upon this show. It had just won the 1990 Tony Award for Best Musical (with wins in other categories, too), my stint at **CAT ON A HOT TIN ROOF** was ending, so I ventured over to the Virginia Theatre on 52$^{nd}$ Street and introduced myself to the head usher, a feisty older lady named Martha. She liked me I guess, because she gave me a shift for that coming week. I said I couldn't wait to see the show. "You wanna watch or you wanna work?" Like I said, feisty.

Yeah, I wanted to work, and I did, for over a year on and off. I met some great people at the Virginia, including an usher named Lolly, who once had been a dancer. She and I would sit on the carpet of the mezzanine, doing our inserts into the *Playbills*. She was still so agile, even at her advancing age. I would later work with her again at her regular house, the Shubert Theatre. She was an early gem of the people I met.

The Virginia became like family, to the point that when my parents came to the city to see the show with my sister Liz and hubby Doug, an incident illustrated just how much. A Saturday night, the five of us had dinner before my shift across the street at Gallagher's Steakhouse. I had to leave early to get to the theatre, putting on my usher uniform and do my inserts. The family arrived, the show began. And then suddenly my mother wasn't feeling well. Liz and I brought her down to the restroom, which back then was manned by a matron.

After my mom was taken care of, she asked Liz if she had anything for a tip. The matron would have none of it. "You're family," she said with pride. Mom missed a lot of the show. The manager was nice enough to invite them back for the Sunday matinee before their train back to Syracuse. We also had dinner afterwards at the Stage Deli, which was re-invented years later as my beloved, and now missed, Stagecoach Tavern.

Memories have a strange way of staying with you. They disappear for a while, I guess in some hidden place in your mind. But when you conjure them, they materialize. My life at **CITY OF ANGELS** is one I'll never forget. Not Martha, not the glamorous Anne taking tickets at the door, not Lolly, not the anniversary party, not New Year's Eve when the new cast came in and leading man (and iconic "Dukes of Hazzard" star) Tom Wopat introduced himself to the front of the house with hearty handshakes.

I still remember those nights. Me, wide-eyed, listening, learning, plotting my own detective stories. The show would close after 879 performances, a good run. I was invited back for the final performance. No seat, just able to stand in the back, but hey, isn't that what I'd done most nights at that show?

Turned out there were angels at the Virginia. On the aisles.

DIARY SEVEN

## The Independents, Part One

Before I took on full-time positions within Shubert, there were a few other of the "independents" that I worked in my early days. This week I'll talk Nederlander-owned houses (they own and/or manage nine of them).

One of the first shows I worked for Nederlander was Neil Simon's **LOST IN YONKERS**, where I got to see the Tony-winning turns of its great cast, led by Mercedes Ruehl and Irene Worth. I worked that show a handful of times, at the newly renamed Richard Rodgers Theatre. It once had the inauspicious name as The 46th Street Theatre. It would be the only show I'd ever work there, but I attended several others, including Matthew Broderick and my then-neighbor Jay in **HOW TO SUCCEED IN BUSINESS WITHOUT REALLY TRYING**. I think...I think, a little-known show called **HAMILTON** resides there now, and probably forever.

Another Nederlander house is the gigantic Gershwin, where I worked a revival of **FIDDER ON THE ROOF** back in 1991, and years later would do a Thanksgiving night shift at the massive hit, **WICKED**. The Gershwin, one of Broadway's more modern houses, built in 1972, is its biggest at 1,933 seats, originally opened as the Uris. Other shows I got tickets for there were **CANDIDE**, **SHOWBOAT**, and **OKLAHOMA**.

Wish I'd seen what they did to that theatre for **STARLIGHT EXPRESS**.

The only time I ever worked the Neil Simon Theatre on 52$^{nd}$ Street was for **HAIRSPRAY**. A Wednesday matinee, and I was up in the mezzanine dealing with many school groups. The things you do to see a show! The Simon was once called the Alvin. I would later see a great revival of **THE MUSIC MAN** and a less-than-great revival of **RAGTIME** at this venue.

Let's move down to 45$^{th}$ Street and the Minskoff. Again, another of the modern theatres, a big barn of a place. My first experience there was not as an usher. I was asked by the union office if I had ever worked as a backstage doorperson. Um, I'd only been ushering for about four weeks, so no. But there I was, working **BLACK AND BLUE**, a musical revue, and my job was to manage the desk at the stage door. Greet the actors and crew, ensure no unauthorized persons entered. At the end of the night, I had to wait for everyone to leave before the porter could lock up all the doors. I've never done that job again. But I did usher **DANCE OF THE VAMPIRES**, and I watched a short-lived Polish-originated musical called **METRO**. Disliked the former, kinda liked the latter and

I'd like to hear the score again. Kind of **RENT** before its time.

Ah, then there's the iconic Palace Theatre. One of the grand showplaces of Broadway, with a storied history that I only experienced once as an usher, for Tommy Tune's dazzling **THE WILL ROGERS FOLLIES**. Still one of my favorite shows, with a star-turn by Keith Carradine and a career-bursting performance by Cady Huffman. That great Cy Coleman score led the way toward many Tony Awards.

Another one of the Nederlander houses I worked only once is over on 47tth Street. the Brooks Atkinson. **JANE EYRE: THE MUSICAL** was playing, and again it was a Wednesday matinee that found me there. I was curious about the show, since I enjoyed the music. I seemed to get to see a lot of shows on mid-week mats—a shift when theatres most relied on sub ushers. Many of us have days jobs. At the time, I was between publishing gigs.

I've discussed the Marquis, since that was the first house I ever worked, but I would return a couple other times. Tyne's **GYPSY** moved to the Marquis prior to their London engagement. I saw **SHOGUN: THE MUSICAL** there (and I liked it; wish there was a recording of that, too.) I've seen a few other shows there like **DAMN YANKEES** with Victor Garber and Bebe Neuwirth, and an ill-fated Frank Wildhorn show called **WONDERLAND**.

The Marquis was also at the center of controversy because its existence is owed to the destruction of three of Broadway's classic theatres: the original Helen Hayes, the Bijou, and the Morosco. Those famous theatres were torn down in the 1980s to build that big Marriot Marquis hotel between 45$^{th}$ Street and 46$^{th}$ Street, its façade facing Broadway. That pre-dated my arrival to New York City, but I would always hear co-workers and friends mention those lost treasures with such affection, perhaps with a bit of remorse.

Then there's the namesake Nederlander Theatre on the outpost of 41$^{st}$ Street. I was asked to work there for the run of a new play called **OUR COUNTRY'S GOOD**, written by Australian playwright Timberlake Wertenbaker. A bit rundown back in the day, a difficult show to sell, a bad location, and seven Tony nominations and no wins got us all a seven-week run. However, I did get to witness the Broadway debut of Cherry Jones (and watch a host of other talented New York stage actors). **RENT** would later take ownership of that theatre for years.

The only Nederlander-owned house I've never ushered: The Lunt-Fontanne on 46$^{th}$ Street. Seen shows there, but that's all. Another beautiful house, named after the iconic married Broadway couple. I could also mention the Mark Hellinger for another stab at theatre lore. **MY FAIR LADY** debuted there and Peter's Allen's **LEGS DIAMOND** was its last show before, in the 1990s it was leased, then eventually sold by the Nederlanders to the Times Square Church.

Broadway is filled with stories of success and regrets, of hit shows and big flops. But each time I went into a theatre I'd never-before worked, I would make sure I was properly dressed, on time, had done my research on the seating chart, and then did what my title dictated, I ushered my patrons to their seats. Then the lights would go down and the show would start. The magic had begun. The history of these theatres ever-present in my mind.

DIARY EIGHT

# The Independents, Part Two

The previous chapter discussed my ushering history with the nine Nederlander houses, so I guess I should continue the theme with the five Jujamcyn-owned theatres. If you're not familiar with their now-familiar "J" logo, the company name is an amalgam of the owner's three children: Judy, James, Cynthia. Kinda clever.

I've mentioned my association with the Eugene O'Neill, the St. James, and Virginia theatres already with specific shows that I worked. But my time at those houses went beyond **CAT ON A HOT TIN ROOF**, **GYPSY**, and **CITY OF ANGELS**.

So, let's go back in time to the early-to-mid 90s. Jujamcyn was producing and housing many shows that pushed Broadway forward. A mix of new shows and revivals with a fresh vision of what a Broadway show could and should be, I always looked forward to getting a shift at one of their theatres. Though, in truth, I only ever worked three of the five.

The Eugene O'Neill on 49th Street. After **CAT** closed, a new show came in, an ambitious play called **LA BETE**, written entirely in iambic pentameter. It included a 20-minute monologue in Act I for actor Tom McGowan in what became a Tony-nominated performance. Sheer brilliance. This was the first time that I was asked to be a ticket taker, and it was on Opening Night, working alongside Bill, the theatre's longtime TT. It was a Sunday night, and I eagerly awaited the reviews on the local news when I got back to my apartment. Reviews were mixed, but a tough sell and an no big stars, the show didn't last. People missed out on that. (It was revived years later at the Music Box with David Hyde-Pierce.)

I also worked Penn & Teller's **THE REFRIGERATOR TOUR** many times. Literally pure magic on that stage, such fun to watch nightly. I would attend other shows at the O'Neill, including a short-lived play called **THE HERBAL BED** with Laila Robins (which I liked but no one else seemed to), the British-import **FIVE GUYS NAMED MOE**, and later, the Tony-winning **SPRING AWAKENING**. **THE BOOK OF MORMON** lives there now. The O'Neill was originally called the Forrest Theatre and later the Coronet.

Let's return to the St. James on 44th Street. Jujamcyn's largest house at over 1,600 seats. I was asked to work a new musical called **THE SECRET GARDEN**, based on the classic novel. A Wednesday matinee, they were expecting LOTS of school groups and were in need of a third ticket taker—an unusual move at the time. I took the assignment but didn't get to see the show that day. I had to get back to my day job. Later that week, I ushered it and... well, it remains one of my most favorite shows ever and for sure, it's lush score by Lucy Simon. I would see other shows at the St. James: **TOMMY, FORUM, GYPSY** (this time with Ms. Lupone), and **AMERICAN IDIOT**.

Now let's head back up to $52^{nd}$ Street and return to the Virginia Theatre. After **CITY OF ANGELS** closed, **JELLY'S LAST JAM** booked the house, and I had the pleasure to work it several times. Watching those Tony-winning performances from Gregory Hines and Tonya Pinkins was electric, and a young Savion Glover tearing up the stage with his gravity-defying dancing was just a preview of his talent. Great score, jazzy and tuneful, a telling true-life story of Jelly Roll Morton. To me, the success of a musical always lies with the book.

I'd also work, once on a Sunday matinee, a revival of **MY FAIR LADY** starring TV-icon Richard Chamberlin and featuring the debut of the luminous Melissa Errico as Eliza. What a voice. Then came **SMOKEY JOE'S CAFÉ** for a long run. Terrific cast and classic songs! It would be the longest-running show in that theatre's history... but that record wouldn't hold.

The theatre would later be renamed the August Wilson, after the famous, award-winning playwright, even though he had only one of his plays produced at this house: **KING HEDLEY III**. **JERSEY BOYS** settled in for a nice 10-year run at this theatre and gained the distinction to become the longest-running show in the history of the Anta/Virginia/Wilson. It took the smoke right out of Joe's Café like those boys had ordered a Taylor ham sandwich from it.

The only two Jujamcyn theatres I've never worked as an usher are the Walker Kerr and the Al Hirschfeld. But I saw shows there. The Kerr had **DOUBT**, **PROOF**, both big hits, **TAKE ME OUT**, another hit, and more recently, **SPRINGSTEEN ON BROADWAY**, a massive hit. Yeah, they get good shows there. It was originally called The Ritz.

As for the Hirschfeld, well, it was for most of its existence the Martin Beck Theatre. I saw the definitive revival of **GUYS AND DOLLS** there (after opening night it made the front page of the *New York Times*, a rare feat), with Nathan Lane and Faith Prince. **WONDERFUL TOWN** with Donna Murphy, **MAN OF LA MACHA** with Brian Stokes Mitchell, **KISS ME KATE** (again with Stokes and the amazing Marin Mazzie), **CURTAINS** with David Hyde Pierce, and my first there, the dance-happy but ultimately tragic and beautiful **GRAND HOTEL** (I got a tour of the stage after the show from the doorman, a friend of mine).

I would move on from these great theatres, but always keeping my *Playbill*s as reminders of such great shows I'd been lucky enough to see. But I mostly remember those nights, whether sitting on the stairs as an employee or sitting in a seat as a patron, marveling at the talent on the stage and the dedication of the house employees. Jujamcyn gave me most of my work when I first started out, and it contributed to a lifelong thrill of working on Broadway. So much for me saying "I'll just do this for six months."

## DIARY NINE

# The Boys from Syracuse

What do Sam & JJ Shubert have in common with me? Why, we're all from Syracuse, New York, but somehow maybe way out west we all found ourselves on the Great White Way. They formed a company bearing their name, but tragedy would strike the brothers. The result is a lasting legacy, the company's flagship and namesake theatre, the Sam S. Shubert Theatre.

For someone who worked for the Shubert Organization for 30 years, it's kind of strange I have a remote relationship with this house. I just didn't work there very much. But I do have some stories, so let's climb those stairs back up to the balcony and work our way down.

In an early diary I wrote about how this was the first Broadway house I'd ever see a show in. Of course it was **A CHORUS LINE**, which played on 44th Street from 1977 to 1990, for a total of 6,137 number of performances. But I'd never work it, as it closed just as I was beginning my Broadway career.

What show could possibly follow such a New York tradition? As it turned out, we went from "At the Ballet" to "La Bamba." Yes, the first show to play the Shubert post that singular sensation was **BUDDY: THE BUDDY HOLLY STORY**. No, I didn't work it, as I had not yet begun working for The Shubert Organization. I went with a friend on a Sunday night, and we were seated in the balcony (uh, again) for an Actor's Fund performance, which meant all proceeds went to charity. I always liked doing my part for the community when I could.

I remembered back to my height-fright at **A CHORUS LINE** and this time, the loud music and the way in which the audience was dancing, clapping, jumping up and down joyously alerted my nerves. I wondered about the foundation of this balcony, built way back in 1913. It was a sold-out show, so all 1,460 were rocking. I felt the floor move. A fun, nostalgic night and luckily, no structural damage.

But I would eventually work the Shubert Theatre. My first show? **CRAZY FOR YOU**, a reinvented Gershwin musical based on their classic show **GIRL CRAZY**. Starring Harry Groener (who I knew from an odd sitcom called "Dear John" and Jodi Benson, the voice of "The Little Mermaid," it became a huge hit and play for 1,622 performances, enhanced by Susan Stroman's inventive choreography.

I had a chance to see the show in previews, my friends having been given comps. For some reason, and

I don't know why (did I have a shift somewhere else? Or just not wanting to have a busman's holiday on a Saturday night?), I skipped out on it. Then it opened and got rave reviews and went on to win the Tony for Best Musical. Not revival. It had been substantially changed from its original incarnation, at least enough so to satisfy the rules from the American Theatre Wing and Tony voters.

But then I got assigned there. I enjoyed the show very much and was given several weeks of ushering work here subsequently. Mostly assigned in the balcony (again!), which still gave me jitters. Eventually I made it down to the mezzanine, but that came with its own issues. There were sight line problems, particularly from the last two rows, which were hindered by the balcony overhang. I recall seeing people having to crook their necks to see the final moment when Harry and Jodi were lifted high above the stage on that wedding cake.

Their heads were cut off from view.

And some patrons would complain to me as they exited the theatre. Not my fault.

The other show I would work at the Shubert, and this one more often, was the hot revival of **CHICAGO**. I first saw it as a patron, scoring house seats at the last minute on a Thursday night. Still featuring the original cast, Bebe, Anne, James, Joel. More of a staged concert than a full-blown production, but it didn't matter to me or the rest of the sold-out crowd. That orchestra was awesome, right there on the stage, playing those jazzy, breezy, horn-blasted tunes. I would work there for a couple of months.

One night, it was a February, was the annual Kid's Night on Broadway, an industry-wide event that had a special ticket deal for patrons. One full-price ticket got a kid under 16 in for free. I guess other deals were available, because that night I was working the balcony and up comes a large school group, teenagers but not quite high schoolers. I pondered the appropriateness of the show for them. Sure, **CHICAGO** is pure razzle dazzle and witty and biting, but it also has a bit of a mixed moral message. Kids might not get its sardonic wit.

Next up for me at the Shubert was a rare Monday night shift, a late-afternoon call to work **GYPSY** starring Bernadette Peters as Mama Rose. Turned out not to be my favorite production of this normally great show. My big takeaway that day was I'd been on a date, which I had to cut short because of that call to work. He thought it was an excuse to end the date early. Not the case. As I've said, you get offered a shift, you don't say no. Still, we dated all summer. I think we lasted longer than that production of **GYPSY**.

I would miss several shows at the Shubert. **BIG: THE MUSICAL**, **BLITHE SPIRIT** with Angela Lansbury. I was lucky enough to be given one matinee shift there for **MONTY PYTHON'S SPAMALOT**, which I was eager to see. It was an Easter Sunday, and I had a free afternoon and many of the regular ushers had taken off for the holiday.

Lucky me. I got to see Tim Curry, David Hyde Pierce, Hank Azaria, and the breakthrough Tony-winning performance of Sara Ramirez. I'd later work the show again, this time with Marin Mazzie (she comes up a lot!) as the Lady of the Lake. Completely ridiculous fun and still a great score to listen to. **SPAMALOT** was a huge hit, winning three Tonys, including Best Musical and Best Director for Mike Nichols.

The most recent show I'd seen at the Shubert Theatre was an Actor's Fund performance of **MEMPHIS**. A decent production, not ground-breaking, but it would win the Tony for Best Musical during what most declared was a lackluster season for musicals. I still liked it, lots of high energy.

So, while I've had limited engagements and opportunities at the Shubert Theatre, you know that old adage? You never forget your first time. It's what I did for love, all the way from Syracuse.

DIARY TEN

## Disorder in the Cort

Sigh. A year. A year since our lights went dark and Broadway closed and our lives and livelihoods changes. Thursday, March 12<sup>th</sup>, 2020, with the matinee of **THE PHANTOM OF THE OPERA**; fitting, I suppose. But for most of us, the news of our closure came on Wednesday, March 11<sup>th</sup>, the last time I had worked a show and the last time I'd even been to New York City.

In honor of this unprecedented year, I share memories and love for the last theatre at which I worked. The Cort. Commissioned in 1912 by impresario John Cort. the Cort Theatre is located on West 48<sup>th</sup> Street, one of the few houses found east of Broadway. Not the most desirable of theatres and off the heavily trafficked paths of 44<sup>th</sup> and 45<sup>th</sup> streets, it still has a storied history all its own, and I have been fortunate to be a small part of its theatrical lore. It's never had another name, thankfully. I like when history still breathes.

**THE MINUTES,** a new play by Pulitzer Prize and Tony-winning playwright Tracy Letts (**AUGUST, OSAGE**

COUNTY) was set to open at the Cort, and I'd been asked by the office to be the second ticket taker for the run of the show. We were scheduled to have our official Opening Night on March 15th, a Sunday night, after a few weeks of previews. Yeah, that opening never transpired, the same situation for several new shows that were coming in that 2020 spring season.

But as, of this writing, we have reached this year-long intermission, and I reflect on my life working at the Cort for many other shows. With its beautiful Versailles-esque architecture and the bust of Marie Antoinette, this under-appreciated house has, well, housed many transcendent and influential shows. It's had its share of flops, too. But, hey, what house hasn't?

My first time working the Cort was for a play called **THE HEIRESS**, a Lincoln Center Theater production starring a then-unknown Cherry Jones. Well, that performance changed all that, her life and the history of the Cort. I worked that show for eight weeks before I was to return to my regular gig at the Barrymore. An amazing production, highlighted not just by Ms. Jones but by the lovely Frances Sternhagen (Cliff Clavin's mom on "Cheers" as I knew her!). A sold-out hit and lots of Tonys ensued.

I would go on to sub at the Cort for several other shows. **MARLENE** starring Welsh star Sian Phillips, **AN AMERICAN DAUGHTER**, a Wendy Wasserstein play that kinda flopped, **THE 39 STEPS**, an inventive interpretation of Alfred Hitchcock's classic innocent-man-accused movie. I'd see other shows as a patron: **THE LITTLE DOG LAUGHED**, with a Tony-winning performance by Julie White; a revival of **BORN YESTERDAY** (Opening Night, and I got to go to the party at the Edison Ballroom!) with Nina Arianda and Jim Belushi. Belushi played with the band.

One of my favorite memories of working the Cort was the ridiculous, fun, frat-boy pleasing one-man show **YOU'RE WELCOME AMERICA: A FINAL NIGHT WITH GEORGE W. BUSH**, starring comedy star Will Ferrell as the freshly departed president. I'll never forget his entrance that first preview, coming down from the rafters, as though he'd just been dropped off by Marine One. The first show coincided with his last day in the White House. The timing was perfect, and intentional. Working center orchestra, I got a $5 dollar tip that first night, and those didn't stop for the entire run. Can we run longer than eight weeks, please?

Here's a fun story about that show. HBO was set to film it for a live broadcast on a Saturday night, a late 9:00 pm show. The night before, they filmed the show, kind of using it as a back-up in case of technical issues on the actual broadcast night. The bar was open that Friday night, and the audience was dropping down bills for many beers and spirits. They were ready to laugh, and laugh they did, loudly. It was a great response to this silly show. Then came the Saturday night performance, the live broadcast. No bar that night, I guess to keep the audience in check, and sorry to say, it was kind of a dud of a show. Will Ferrell's quirky and funny interpretation of 43 required beers to elicit the big laughs.

I've seen and worked other shows at the Cort, but those get their own entries, long stories with big stars. For now, I want to thank the Cort Theatre and my east of Broadway friends for my early experiences, and for those final, but troubled weeks before the shutdown. It's a beautiful old theatre, three levels (yeah, that balcony is high!), with 1082 seats.

But to realize who stood on that stage and, yeah, who worked that house, gives me such appreciation. No matter what your role is on Broadway, the curtain doesn't go up without us all working together. Let us hope that soon the curtain soon goes up again, and that we also share the joy, the cries, the laughter, the mutual experience of, sure, a life upon the stage. But one that reflects at us, too, maybe with a sense of hope as the lights go down.

CODA: As I edit this book, it was just announced that the Cort Theatre will be renamed after the legend (Tony-winner and the voice of Darth Vader!), James Earl Jones. A lovely honor to a man of theater.

DIARY ELEVEN

## Ghostly Memories

I can't believe it's taken eleven entries for me to discuss… the Belasco Theatre. Or, as I call it, my spiritual Broadway home. No other theatre has had such an impact on me, my life, my Broadway career and my appreciation for what theatre means then this historic building.

The year is 1907, and on 44th Street, closer to Sixth Avenue then to Broadway and the rest of the community, opened the Stuyvesant, built by impresario David Belasco. He would have named it after himself, but he already had a Belasco Theatre on the corner of 42nd Street and 7th Avenue. That place is now named the New Victory, an off-Broadway house.

The Belasco became the famed Belasco Theatre in 1910. Broadway's second oldest, still-running legit house (the Lyceum is the first—stay tuned, I've got a few stories about that place). The Belasco and I have many stories, it more than me. But the first thing I can speak to is the balcony entrance. See, if you bought tickets for the third level, you had to enter by a separate door. I worked it for years, both the door and the aisles upstairs, and patrons seemed so offended by not being able to enter the theatre by the front doors.

Here's the story, as I understand it. It was the age of segregation and black and white audiences were not allowed to mingle together, let alone sit next to each other. Belasco crafted the separate balcony entrance to include the, as it sometimes called now, the "minority" crowd. But he possessed such forethought during his era, being inclusive for the time-period and progressive in wanting to share the joy of the stage with everyone. No matter race, color or gender. A man with thoughts, an awareness, of where our future was heading.

How did I come to the Belasco? After one shift at the Broadway (the original production of **MISS SAIGON**), a woman named Katie who was filling in there would become the chief usher at the soon-to-reopen Belasco. It had been closed for a couple years, so they needed staff to fill the aisles. I was asked by her, and by the Shubert office, if I would like a spot there. Since I'd only been with Shubert for a couple of months, I welcomed the chance to have "a house." Regular work, week after week.

I was assigned to the balcony, two ushers up there to cover the aisles. A new colleague and I, Michael, who was never without his guitar case adorning his back. We would switch aisles each week, house left or house right, just to keep things interesting up there. I mean, we were in our own world high up in the theatre. Except for Pat, the ticket taker who worked the door downstairs. I loved working with her. I'll always remember when a gentleman came up those (many) stairs and I asked how I could help him. Turned out, he was a bigwig at my company, the Shuberts. I passed the test and received praise from my immediate boss for my ability to handle the crowd and know the seating.

But hey, let's get back to the shows. What was playing there? It was the first season of Tony Randall's dream, the National Actor's Theatre, a repertory company that would produce and perform a seasons worth of plays. Ambitious and exciting and buzz-worthy, we were sold out for much of the run of the first show. Arthur Miller's **THE CRUCIBLE,** starring Martin Sheen.

I remember one night Mr. Sheen couldn't go on, so Mr. Randall stepped in. But he didn't know the lines, so he walked around the set with the script in hand, speaking when it was his turn. Now that's live theatre! Mr. Randall addressed the audience prior to curtain to explain what was going on. What was going on was the role usually played by Felix Unger would be played by John Proctor. A singular odd couple for the ages.

The second of the three productions was a French farce, Feydeau's **A LITTLE HOTEL ON THE SIDE,** featuring among others, Rob Lowe. It was fun and silly. He was good, actually, and I enjoyed watching it. It gave me an appreciation for farce that later became the hallmark of the sitcom "Frasier." Watch the Ski Lodge episode with Guy!

Then came the third production of the season, Ibsen's **THE MASTER BUILDER**, directed by Mr. Randall. While I am trying to keep my diary positive, this was probably one of the worst things I've seen performed and directed on the stage. Lynn Redgrave did her best, but the show was dull and lackluster and, well, lazy. Or, just bad. Encompassing three acts (which means two intermissions), our audience size dwindled as the night dragged on. My mantra? Never give an audience two chances to leave a production.

But back to the Belasco itself. In the early 90s, it was much maligned for not being a house of hits, maligned for its rundown nature and history of...well, flops. It was a last resort theatre for producers. But I loved it. Yeah, it was old and it was creaky, but when you researched and read its history, you realized you were in the presence of a piece of Broadway's past few got to see.

I would eventually work my way down from the balcony, to first the mezzanine, and finally center orchestra. But the NAT season was coming to a close and they would move next season to the Lyceum. But I still wanted to keep working. Most of our staff was transferred to another theatre that was re-opening: the Golden, which back then wasn't booked often. So, they needed a whole new staff. Katie the chief taking most of us over from the Belasco. It's a small playhouse on West

45th Street at only 805 seats but it would go on to great success with a bunch of shows, More on that theatre later in a later diary.

So many stories at this iconic theatre, too! I'd return several times to the Belasco over the years, enjoying big hits and epic flops. I'll tell more in future entries. For now, just know…the Belasco is held firm in my heart for not just so many shows, not just so many memories, but one particular tug at my heart that bonded theatre with family. Stay tuned.

DIARY TWELVE

## A Night with the Lyceum

I consider myself Mr. East of Broadway. I've recounted days at the Cort and the Belasco. So, hey, let's stay there, and head to 45<sup>th</sup> Street between 6<sup>th</sup> and 7<sup>th</sup> Avenues, to the Lyceum Theatre, the oldest currently operating theatre in Broadway history. I've worked there...oh, so many times I can't count how many. There's something special about entering the stage door on 46<sup>th</sup> Street and knowing you're playing even a small part in theater history.

The beautiful Lyceum. Built in 1903, it is again, one of those theatres with three levels, orchestra, mezzanine, balcony, and aside from the St. James, probably has the highest balcony of all the 41 theatres, with a scary (to me) incline. And lots of steps to get up there, winding staircases to conjure Hitchcock's "Vertigo." But with its impressive façade, its wood-lined orchestra walls, the fabulous "cigar room" in the basement where one of the bars is situated, the Lyceum itself is worth the price of admission.

I spent a lot of time in the Lyceum's lobby when I was named its ticket taker during a Lincoln Center-produced show called **THE NANCE** by Douglas Carter Beene, starring Nathan Lane. As a single ticket-taker house, I was "late" every night, meaning I worked till the end of the show eight times a week. This was my first full-time TT gig, and I loved it. The box office staff and manager became great associates. And friends. They were very welcoming to me; we made a good team.

I first came to the Lyceum in the 90s, when the staff from the Barrymore was transferred there after our show had closed. Our new show? **THE SCHOOL FOR SCANDAL**, a National Actor's Theatre production, part of their second season after having switched theatres from the Belasco. Seems Tony Randall and I were destined to still work together. I would also work NAT's **SAINT JOAN**; I remember reading manuscripts for my publishing job on the mezzanine stairs while the show played on. I couldn't watch it every night! Then there was **IS HE DEAD**, a newly discovered play by Mark Twain, and later, **THE PLAY THAT GOES WRONG**; the powerful **THE SCOTTSBORO BOYS**; Julia Sweeney's **AND GOD SAID HA**, and the brilliant, Tony-winning **I AM MY OWN WIFE** starring Tony-winner Jefferson Mays (I would work that show every Wednesday matinee for several months).

With the Belasco under renovation, I was asked to head back to the Lyceum in 2009 for a Lincoln Center production called **IN THE NEXT ROOM (OR THE VIBRATOR PLAY)**. Yeah, I know, that title, but that's how it was billed. I was still ushering then, and I worked every aisle and level during its run; I will admit, even with stars like Laura Benanti and Michael Cerveris, it ranks among my least favorite shows I've ever worked (or seen). Act II should never be longer than Act I! We'd come down at 8:50 for intermission, then end the show (with a naked Cerveris) at 10:35.

Back to **THE NANCE**, and one of my most memorable experiences on Broadway. It was a Sunday matinee and I'm scanning tickets, directing patrons to their aisles, when around 2:45, I heard a woman scream from upstairs, "Oh my God, he fell out the window." Indeed, a patron on the mezzanine level had taken a rest on a chair in the outer mezzanine lobby, right near the bay windows that looked out on 45th Street, while his wife got them infrared listening devices. Not sure of all the details on how this unfortunate event unfolded, but the window behind the man became unclasped. He leaned back in the chair, and next thing we know...he'd fallen out and onto the top of the marquee!

First of all, the gentleman was fine. Thankfully. Secondly, our security guy Joe ran up the stairs and in true super-hero fashion leaped onto the marquee to help the fallen man. The fire department came quickly and got the patron down with the aid of a cherry picker. Talk about drama! The manager was busy supervising the situation, so she instructed me that at 3:05, the show should start. It was the only time I've ever had the privilege to tell stage management, "you have the house." Extraordinary circumstances call for unique situations. The couple would return to see the show another day, this time with seats in the orchestra.

It took less than 15 minutes for colleagues from other theatres to text me and ask what had happened. News travels fast in this world we call Broadway. It's quite the insular community.

**THE NANCE** closed that August, though we did spend a couple days that next week while it was being filmed for PBS. I would return a less than a month later to the Lyceum for its next show, **A NIGHT WITH JANIS JOPLIN**; great performances for sure, but the music was so loud, I wasn't sure that old balcony could survive the excitement of the audience! Great Opening Night party at Planet Hollywood next door, where I made friends with a couple of the producers. That was the thing about being the TT, you made different connections with the creative staff than you did being on the aisle. I was having a blast. But I would only stay with the show for a couple more weeks, because as it turned out, the Belasco was once again calling me to its doors.

The Lyceum's first-ever production was **THE PROUD PRINCE**. Obviously, I wasn't there for Opening Night a century ago, but I'm thrilled to be among the proud princes of this theatre's illustrious history.

DIARY THIRTEEN

## The Tony That Got Away

It's almost like we're stuck in an endless east of Broadway time loop, because we're still here, or back here. I still felt like the King of East of Broadway. And there's a good reason for our return trip to my favorite place in New York City, the Belasco Theatre. Because sometimes, your journey takes you to the **END OF THE RAINBOW**. A pot of gold awaited…well, almost.

**END OF THE RAINDOW**, a musical play written by Peter Quilter, began previews at the Belasco on March 19, 2012, and officially opened on April 2. I'd returned there, yet again, this time in a role we in the front of house called "director." Not of the show, of course, but of helping the patrons get to their seats. I didn't work an aisle, I was the greeter inside the front door on the orchestra level, ensuring everyone was headed to the correct aisle and knew where the bathrooms and bar and merchandise were located. Sort of a concierge of Broadway.

**END OF THE RAINDOW** was about the last days of Judy Garland as she attempted a series of concerts in London, and our leading lady was a brilliant powerhouse British actress named Tracie Bennett. Or, as I called her, Ms. Bennett. I remember that first night of previews, watching that performance and wondering if I was the only one seeing sheer ownership of a stage and a role when Tony-winner and an actress I'd worked with on a show (more on that in another diary), came up to me at intermission and said, 'How can she possibly do this eight times a week?"

It was Judith Light.

And Ms. Light had just seen what I'd seen: the Act I closer, "The Man That Got Away."

Well, she asked a good question, especially coming from such an acclaimed actress herself. You knew you were witnessing something special. Ms. Bennett never missed a show, eight times a week for the next six months, the most powerhouse performance I'd ever seen. I felt bad for her understudy, a very nice and talented actress named Sarah Uriate Berry, whom I'd worked with on **TABOO**. But back to Ms. Bennett. She had to act, chew scenery, sing the crap out of those classic songs, all in high heels and an energy that wouldn't abate for two-plus hours.

The opening night party was held at the legendary Plaza Hotel, and for sure as shit it was one fancy-ass event. Just talking foul like she would! The champagne flowed like it was liquid gold, the food was delicious and indulgent. It was one of those parties where cast, crew, front of house, all were truly invested in the want of a success of a show. We were all in this together, not separated by front and backstage. Ms. Bennett our binder.

Now, I try not to be a name-dropper as a way to impress, but for this show…I've got a few fun encounters. As "director," sometimes I took care of the VIPs as they arrived, and we had a lot of them coming to see Ms. Bennett. I greeted former baseball manager Joe Torre and escorted him to his seat; Elaine Stritch needed to use the accessible restroom on the main level and I walked her over there, her arm wrapped in mine as I walked her there and back.

But then there was one special night. I had four very VIPs coming to see the show, and I had arranged great seats for them. My then 85-year-old mother (she's 94 as of this writing) and my three fabulous sisters, all of them enjoying a couple of days of fun in New York City. Their home base? My theatre district haunt: West 44th Street. They stayed at the Millennium Hotel, they (me too!) dined at the late, lamented Saju Bistro (one of my favorites, thanks Olga, Kevin, Jean-Marc), and then they came across the street to the Belasco to see **END OF THE RAINBOW**. They were greeted by the manager and staff as though royalty had arrived, and you know what? That couldn't have more true in my book. My mother had never been to the Belasco, but she knew how much it meant to me. To have the two finally meet? Ideal.

My sister Peggy spoke up, knowing we were a buzzy show: "Do you think there will be any celebrities in the audience tonight?" Almost like she conjured this night from a single wish.

Here's what happened. The four of them were seated center orchestra, I think row G on the aisle. Thanks to the box office staff for their help in securing these awesome seats! But even better, who sits in front of them? Martin Short, Andrea Martin, Victor Garber, Paul Shaffer, Eugene Levy. But on the other center aisle was Joan Rivers, and at intermission as I was walking down the aisle Ms. Rivers stopped me (we had met before and she was always lovely and a huge theatre fan), and asked me who else was here, since she was going backstage and wanted a heads-up of whom she'd have to greet. I pointed to the other side of the orchestra level, and as she looked noticed someone in the middle of a nearby row.

"Is that Isabella Rossellini? Oh, she looks terrible." This, from Joan Rivers. Insert your own caption. My sister Peggy remarked to me after the show, "Were you talking to Joan Rivers?" Yeah, I was. I love this story.

Okay, one more insider tale of **RAINBOW**. Each night, my manager Stephanie and I would stand at the back of the theatre at the end of the show, wondering if there would be an encore. You never knew from night to night, it was always up to Ms. Bennett…until we figured out her pattern. During the curtain call, if Ms. Bennett came out still in her heels, the audience got their encore.

If she came out sans-heels, no encore and the curtain came down. Show over.

Tracie Bennett would go on to get a Tony nomination for her performance (she was totally robbed of the win, she was just f-ing awesome), but she would win the Drama Desk and Outer Critics Circle awards, as well as a Theatre World Award in an afternoon ceremony that took place at the Belasco. I got to work that and see her accept her award.

Every night when I would arrive to work, I would see Ms. Bennett in the side alley, near the stage door smoking a cigarette or just hanging out, and I would greet her, always calling her Ms. Bennett. That's respect! When the show played its final performance in August of that year, too early as far as I was concerned, there was an informal closing night party across the street at The Long Room pub. I got a chance to thank Ms. Bennett for her amazing performance and for lighting up the Belasco stage. Her response?

"Would you please call me Tracie?"

Nope, I couldn't. It was our thing. All I could do was take a final bow and cheer her with a beer. But with Tracie and Judy and the Belasco, there was no place like home.

DIARY FOURTEEN

# Waiting for the Fat Lady to Sing

Let's go back in time, shall we, to a more innocent time when theatre and live performances influenced my eventual Broadway life. See, I always enjoyed singing and I had a decent enough voice, a tenor masquerading as an alto at a teenage year. Hey, we're talking 7$^{th}$ grade, my voice hadn't changed just yet. I was kind of like Peter Brady.

I tried out for the Eagle-Hill Middle School chorale, and my audition song was an odd choice, The "John B Sails" by the Beach Boys. But its notes fit my vocal range and the choir director, Mr. Goldberg, told me I sounded great, despite the fact I thought I sounded nasally from a cold. He said, "keep it." I was accepted into the program. At a spring outdoor concert, I was asked to perform a solo, and I chose (yeah, you can laugh at my choice, but I loved it) Leo Sayer's chart-topper "When I Need You." It was a big hit back then and I was told by a friend's mother that I had perfect pitch. Okay, I'll take that!

I still possess, in a cardboard box of nostalgic items, the sheet music which I bought at Camelot Music at the Fayetteville Mall. Just across the way from Waldenbooks. I would frequent both stores often. Music and books, those infatuations began at any early age. I had also bought the 45 RPM recording of that song there, too, for $1.27, and still own it along with all my other singles. I have index cards of all the songs I bought over those teen years. OCD? Um, yeah.

But pop music would have to take a break for a bit, as the unlikely world of…wait for it, opera took over. Opera?

See, the two choir directors from F-M, Mr. Goldberg and Mr. Campbell, from the middle school and high school respectively, were well connected in the music world of Central New York. The Syracuse Civic Center was putting on a production of Georges Bizet's **CARMEN**, and they needed a cadre of boys to play the street urchins at the top of the show. I was selected as one of those boys! My professional debut, as a legit theatre.

**CARMEN** was first performed in 1875 and continues to be one of the most-produced operas of all time. What a joy it was to sing and hear that memorable score, live and in front of an audience. The "Toreador Song" was among its most memorable pieces. Don't spit on the floora.

We rehearsed the music and staging at the black box studio in downtown Syracuse for a couple of weekends, and then it was time for performances. The curtain came up on the boys, all of us downstage, kicking around a ball while the orchestra played the memorable overture. The show was only scheduled for a handful of performances, but I do remember one of those shows we accidentally sent the ball sailing into the orchestra pit. Oops. Like a soccer match gone wrong.

I got to perform in another staging the next year, this time for the operetta **HANSEL AND GRETEL**, written by German composer Engelbert Humperdinck. No, not the 70's singer! The show premiered in 1893. Again, a troop of boys were cast, this time to play the victims of that wily witch. There was a stretch of time during the show where we all had to stand with our arms, well, outstretched, as though we had been transformed into trees. We had to hold that pose for 20 minutes. A challenge for a thirteen-year-old who didn't like to sit still.

That box of nostalgia contains programs from both shows. But I remember **CARMEN** was between my $7^{th}$ and $8^{th}$ grade, **HANSEL AND GRETEL** I guess the next year, during my $8^{th}$ grade year. It was the beginning of a love affair with music, whether theatre, musical, opera, or pop and rock.

Another memorable experience early on was when our high school chorale got to record an album. We went into a recording studio in Syracuse and laid down tracks for songs in a variety of musical styles. We did pop/rock. Like "Black Water" by the Doobie Brothers, and "Tin Man" by America; we did some standards, some show tunes, fugues and even madrigals. I've recently reclaimed that album from storage and laughed a lot while playing it.

But this story brings me back to the idea of opera. How does that form impact my Broadway world, a place built on plays and musicals?

Well, first, there's **CARMEN JONES**, based on Bizet's opera, with an assist by Oscar Hammerstein II. It played the Broadway Theatre in 1943. Then we move to **PORGY AND BESS**, the Gershwin's masterpiece, which can be performed as either musical theatre or opera and has been done so over the years. Its last appearance on Broadway was staged at the Richard Rodgers Theatre, with Audra McDonald and Norm Lewis, winning the Tony for Best Musical Revival. I saw a different, and less successful, production of it at the Savoy Theatre in London.

Broadway has also not been short on what is referred to as "rock operas." Think **JESUS CHRIST SUPERSTAR**, revived a couple of times on Broadway, most recently at the Neil Simon Theatre. **THE WHO'S TOMMY** at the St. James (saw it on my 30th birthday!); there was a recent concert at the Broadway Theatre called **ROCKTOPIA**, which combined contemporary music with orchestral classics; I worked a few performances. And of course, the brilliant play **MASTER CLASS** by Terrence McNally, about opera star Maria Callas won accolades and awards. I got to work that show at the Golden a few times, watching

Tony winning performances by Zoe Caldwell and Audra McDonald.

Then there's **RENT**, based on Puccini's **LA BOHEME**. I saw that show a few times down at the Nederlander; still love listening to the score. And finally, there's **LA BOHEME** itself; well, a modern-day staging of the classic opera, directed by the innovative filmmaker Baz Luhrmann of **MOULIN ROUGE** fame. I got to work that show one night, again, at the Broadway Theatre. My first time seeing the awesome Alfie Boe live. More on him another time

For now, I guess the fat lady has sung.

## DIARY FIFTEEN

# Indiscreet Sisters, Husbands, and Sushi

We're headed west of Broadway for this trip down memory lane, where most of the theatres are located. In fact, let's go to 47$^{th}$ Street, and head to the beautiful Ethel Barrymore Theatre. Named after the famed and acclaimed actress, built specifically for her by the Shubert brothers.

The Barrymore opened its doors in 1928 and has been home to so many shows over the decades. Mostly known as a playhouse, it has on occasion featured several musicals as well. My experience with the Barrymore began in 1993, with the Lincoln Center Theater production of Wendy Wasserstein's acclaimed **THE SISTERS ROSENSWEIG**. After a sold-out run at the off-Broadway Mitzi Newhouse Theatre on 65$^{th}$ Street, it transferred with fanfare to Broadway. Starring Jane Alexander, Robert Klein, and the incomparable Madeline Kahn, it was a huge hit.

We had a great front of house staff at the Barrymore, led by Chief Usher Eileen, and fellow ushers Anthony, Ronnie, Caroline, Mark, Daria, Aileen, ticket taker Mr. Banks, and our manager Dan. We were a tight-knit group and worked really well together. I remember how we would all munch down on cinnamon Mentos prior to opening the doors to our patrons. The box office staff was also super friendly, led by its treasurer Bill.

I was assigned to center orchestra, house-right, working alongside my new coworker and pal Anthony. We were a great team, working in tandem to get hundreds of people to their seats in the half-hour timeframe we had. We also had to handle the side aisle, since back then there was no usher manning it. We would have to direct patrons to the last aisle and tell them to go through the curtains to find rows E, F. G, and back then the metal seat placards were on the arm, not the seat, so there was a lot of confusion for the patrons. The Barrymore was a house of 1,058 seats, but only had eight ushers. Two shy of what it should have been.

I recall a night when my parents came to visit the city. While they were more prone to seeing musicals, I encouraged them to see **ROSENSWEIG**. Ms. Kahn's performance was not to be missed, she just nailed that role as Dr. Gorgeous Teitelbaum. Her scene in Act II about the shoes stole the show. I secured my folks seats in the back row of the orchestra and suggested they might like to use our available infrared listening system to enhance their enjoyment of the show. They complied, and it made a big difference. I loved watching them laugh at the lines I knew so well.

"The shoes!"

But all shows end, and the next attraction to come to the Barrymore was an unlikely play called **INDISCRETIONS**, starring Kathleen Turner, Roger Rees, Eileen Atkins, with supporting roles by the then little-known Cynthia Nixon and Jude Law (who appeared naked at one point in the show as he emerged from a bathtub at the start of Act II). It was a crazy script, but beautifully staged by its director Sean Mathias, with an amazing second act spiral staircase.

**INDISCRETIONS** was my first ticket-taking experience for an opening night with Shubert. I worked alongside my pal Joe, but soon that night I had to leave. My day job was calling at night. I had a publishing engagement at the same time—the annual Edgar Awards given by the Mystery Writers of America, kind of our Oscars, at a dinner banquet. For which I was very late getting to. Balancing two careers sometimes came with its conflict. An award ceremony and a Broadway opening on the same night? What life was I living? But in the end, I managed to pull off both. One of the books I edited won an award that night.

**INDISCRETIONS** wasn't so lucky, as reviews were mixed. It would be nominated for nine Tony Awards, each actor but Ms. Turner in the running for the prize (which was wrong!), and on the night of the Tonys what was most memorable was that the show won NONE. Not a single one! We ran for eight months, closing in November after our April opening.

The next production I worked at the Barrymore was a classic play written by Oscar Wilde, **AN IDEAL HUSBAND**. Presented by The Peter Hall Company from England, it was an unlikely hit. Funny and witty, we all had fun watching this play and listening to those biting lines unfold night after night. The ushers even wore buttons on our shirts, with sayings like "I am An Ideal Husband' or "I Want an Ideal Husband." Isn't it nice that second button came true!

We ended up getting a replacement cast for that show when the contracts ran out for the British actors, and it was to my extreme pleasure that the role of socialite Mrs. Cheveley would be played by "Dynasty/The Colbys" star Stephanie Beacham. (The recast show also featured Kim Hunter making her Barrymore return after she'd starred on this stage years ago in the initial production of **A STREETCAR NAMED DESIRE**. That's theatre royalty right there.)

But not everything can be ideal in this world. This would end up being my final long run at the Barrymore. Another transfer was in the works, as it happened often in my career. I liked to move around, and in truth if I hadn't this, this book wouldn't exist. This time, I was headed back to my beloved Belasco—more on that story later. But I would make a return to the Barrymore years later, working the first few weeks of previews and the opening of David Mamet's **SPEED THE PLOW** revival, with Jeremy Piven, Raul Esparza, and Elisabeth Moss. As I watched the show, I had this passing thought: there is no way Mr. Piven would last the entire run. He just didn't seem committed to the production.

He would famously and reportedly get mercury poisoning from overdosing on sushi, the story much publicized in the tabloids. He departed the show a couple months into the run. Tony winner Norbert Leo Butz would step into the role, using the script for the first few shows to get through the fast-paced dialogue. William H. Macy came in later, and my friends Phil and Liz, fans of his, got to say hi to him after the show at The Glass Tavern located across the street from the Barrymore on 47th Street.

What I most fondly remember about the Barrymore was a short story I wrote during my time there, a horror/black comedy tale about an usher who takes revenge against rude patrons. It was called **SOME NIGHTS YOUR ONLY FRIENDS ARE CRITICS**, and the staff at the theatre, notably chief Eileen, after reading it, said "You're sick." Sounds like a compliment to me. But then one year I ran a Tony Awards pool, all the staff joining in to select their choices of winners. I watched the show, marking up everyone's ballots. Turned out: um, I won. The staff was suspect of my win. But I swear, there was no monkey business. I read the papers and the gossip columns and see shows and understand the politics behind the Tony committee. It was a fair victory. A new pack of Mentos got me back in their good graces. Paid for with my spoils.

The Barrymore also happens to be neighbor to the legendary (in my fictional world) Harold Calloway Theatre; that's where my Jimmy McSwain's mother Maggie works. Isn't that a curious incident! The Calloway's most recent tenant was the Broadway premiere of Kander and Ebb's revue **AND THE WORLD GOES ROUND**. (Didn't actually happen, but it was fun to mount that production in my pretend world.)

DIARY SIXTEEN

## Anarchy on the Aisles

As the cast sings in **THE PRODUCERS**, "It's opening night!" As I write this diary all of Broadway awaits the return of those special, heightened nights, where paparazzi gather with their cameras, where red carpets are laid out and security steps up their game, where celebrities give the night a shot of glamour. It's fun to think about those halcyon times before the world changed and dark nights became the norm. Usually, the last two weeks of April would see a spate of new shows set to open, almost an opening every night to squeeze in just in time for the obsession that was Tony nomination time. Lots of money was riding on those openings.

Opening Nights on Broadway can be chaotic, hectic. There is a thrilling, anxious sense that pervades the theatre, producers and stage managers and theatre owners running around, making sure every detail is perfect. As though a broken seat in the mezzanine would cause a bad review! (No critic sits in the mezz.) Backstage is frantic, cast members excited to finally open after weeks of previews with their Gypsy robe ceremony; orchestra (if it's a musical) tuning their instruments, wardrobe and stagehands doing their prep work in the bowels of these old theatres. But everyone is dressed up, excited, because they know it's a special night.

For those of us on the front lines—meaning my world, the front of the house—it's a unique experience. I've worked many nights as an usher during openings, many times on center orchestra, which is the busiest section and where we see the most action and the most difficulty. We would usually open the house earlier than normal, say 6:00 for a scheduled 6:45 curtain (which wouldn't go up until 7:00!). People would arrive slowly, because they were outside being photographed or filmed, but then they would start to take their seats. Sort of.

Sure, we would escort them to their down-front seats, but they would rarely sit at the start, too busy were they air-kissing and saying hello to friends and fellow industry people. They usually blocked the aisle while I and my fellow ushers attempted to avert them to direct the newly arriving guests to their seats; all while trying not to drop the stack of *Playbills* in our hands.

Oh, and the *Playbills*. We had to ensure we had the specific Opening Night programs for these performances. On the title page, which listed the show's credits, the cast, of course the producers (often many of them), but at the top of the page is printed the date of the opening. But we were given those stacks of *Playbills* a few days in advance, because they were to be used for what's called "press previews." That's when the critics came, often over the course of a few day prior to the official opening. We often had those "opening night" *Playbills* for weeks, depending upon the reviews.

Openings weren't always like what I encountered. Back before I worked on Broadway, perhaps back even before I was born, critics would attend the actual official opening night, and to keep them sober the producers would make the decision to close the bar for that performance. Then the critics would run back to their newsroom typewriters like they were starring in **THE FRONT PAGE** and bang out their fraught opinions on the show. That practice of closing the bar sometimes still occurs, it's left up to each producer and company; the reviews are now written a few days in advance at those designated press previews.

In my early days at the Belasco, I've written that I worked the balcony exclusively. No celebs us there! But I would have time to peer over that high railing and watch the action unfold before the curtain even went up. I worked so many openings as an usher—three shows for the National Actor's Theatre, **FALSETTOS** at the Golden, the aforementioned shows at the Barrymore; at the Cort, the Lyceum, then back at the Belasco for **JOE TURNER'S COME AND GONE, PASSING STRANGE, WOMEN ON THE VERGE OF A NERVOUS BREAKDOWN.** (More on those shows later.)

Sometimes the front of house staff would be invited to the opening night party. It was always a lingering question, and sometimes we wouldn't find out until the day of the actual opening. Ushers are not always at the front of the line, even if we are at the front of the house. One producer, I won't say who, was known for not being inclusive to house staff. For one show, a fellow usher asked a producer if we were invited to the opening party. The response, sent through our house manager: it would cost us each $75 to attend. We didn't go.

But many other times we got to celebrate with the cast and crew at fancy Manhattan spots, eating yummy food and indulging in the open bar. But the parties were not about the food or drink, it was about us feeling as though we were part of the show's celebration. You don't have a show without first a producer, a theatre owner, a cast, a crew, but ultimately, you've got no audience if not for the front of house staff.

We all do our part to ensure a show's success, and the audience's enjoyment.

DIARY SEVENTEEN

# Don't Change My Name, I'm Good Luck

Okay, let's take a stroll down West 44$^{th}$ this week, to the historic and beautiful Broadhurst Theatre, which sits between the Shubert and the Majestic theatres on the north side of the block. But it is no less grand or desirable than those two iconic houses, and its one with a rich history all its own of famous productions. I've worked there many times over the years.

Built in 1917, it is one of the few Broadway houses which has never changed its name, having been built by George Howells. Broadhurst, an impresario and playwright who lived from 1866 to 1952—not a bad run in and of itself. The Broadhurst remains one of the most sought-after theatres on the Great White Way, suitable for either plays and/or musicals. At 1218 seats, its sightlines are among the best of the theatres for patrons. Even the boxes! (We'll get to those…they are Mahvelous.)

I first came to work the Broadhurst on New Year's Eve in 1997, back when Broadway still had performances on that day. But oddly, it was a matinee, and since I was free that afternoon from my shifts at the Barrymore, I offered to fill in as a substitute usher. It was a production of Neil Simon's **PROPOSALS**, not one of his most successful plays; it opened to lukewarm at best reviews and ran for a mere 76 performances. With an ensemble cast, Broadway vets like Dick Latessa and future Tony winner Katie Finneran, plus a guy from TV I recognized, Matt Letscher, it just didn't, uh, play with critics or audiences.

Aside from working the aisles, I also attended shows at the Broadhurst, too. Andrew Lloyd Webber's **ASPECTS OF LOVE** was supposed to be a big hit, his first new show since **PHANTOM**. I took my young, impressionable composer nephew David with me to the Broadhurst during a visit of his to the city, getting discount tickets from the TKTS booth. He's now an acclaimed composer and writer, with a wife who acts and directs in film and TV. Maybe that show had more aspects than I thought. David developed his first pilot for a drama series on ABC and is never lacking for new ideas and opportunities. Kind of like his uncle!

Another night, I was the odd man out from a company publishing event, an awards ceremony where there were only a select number of tickets. Low man on the totem pole was out. It was a Friday night and as I wasn't scheduled to usher anywhere, since I'd taken the night off for the event, I ended up buying a standing room ticket for Chita Rivera in the new musical **KISS OF THE SPIDER WOMAN**, also featuring Brent Carver and Anthony Crivello. At intermission, I had garnered an aisle seat in the mezzanine; an usher, you know, knows how to work his connections.

I would later work several weeks at **KISS** when Vanessa Williams took over the lead from Chita and I thought she was great. I might have enjoyed it more than the original stars...I know, sacrilege! Sarah Jessica Parker later headlined a very not-funny revival of **ONCE UPON A MATTRESS**, which included a painful scene which went on too long where she rolled all over the mattress because she felt the pea. I blame the director for that scene. Oh, then there was the earnest but just bad **URBAN COWBOY**, which announced their closing shortly after its opening. It got a one-week reprieve from its deep-pocketed (and very sweet and earnest) producer, Chase Mishkin, who surprised her cast by announcing the extension by appearing on stage during the curtain call. The buzz about the extra week didn't really help box office receipts. Talented cast, just not good material.

My next turn working the aisles at the Broadhurst came with **FOSSE**, a musical review of the dances of the iconoclast Bob Fosse. I worked that show for several weeks during previews, and while it's primarily a visual experience, I still enjoy listening to the cast recording and the wonderful orchestrations. "Life is Just a Bowl of Cherries," "Crunchy Granola Suite," "Sing Sing Sing," so many other great songs from **PIPPIN** and **SWEET CHARITY** and others. The music brings memories of that stagecraft to life. It was funny to think that "Nowadays" from **CHICAGO** was being performed as part of the revue of **FOSSE**, while next door at the Shubert **CHICAGO** was playing nightly as well. "Nowadays" next door to each other, that's how you know you wrote a good song. Isn't it great, isn't it grand?

In 2008, I filled in for one night at the buzzy revival of **EQUUS**, starring Harry Potter's own Daniel Radcliffe. Adventurous direction, lots of press attention about him being all grown up (and naked). The production sold a few rows of seats on the stage, raised up behind the unfolding drama. That's where I was stationed, and you had to sit there the entire time, watching the audience watch the show to ensure they didn't take pictures or, worse, distract the actors they were so close to. The ushers were not allowed to give those patrons seated up there *Playbill*s until after the show had ended, thus preventing anyone from accidentally on purpose dropping one on the stage.

Lots of notable actors and names have played the Broadhurst in recent years. Tom Hanks in **LUCKY GUY**, Bruce Willis and Laurie Metcalf in **MISERY**, **THE FRONT PAGE** with Nathan Lane (though he's probably worked almost all the theatres; kinda like me), Richard Griffiths, Jude Law, Al Pacino, and Hugh Jackman. The list goes on and on.

But my longest run at the Broadhurst was by far, and most memorably, **700 SUNDAYS**, written, produced, and starring Billy Crystal. But that show deserves its own entry, and I'll get there later in the book, around page 700. (Just a joke…it's a fun chapter.)

My last full-run at the Broadhurst was the short-lived **LENNON** (some called it **LEMON**), a bio-musical about John Lennon, with the famed singer being portrayed by several actors, both male and female. It was a concept that didn't work (and still doesn't, witness **DONNA SUMMER** and **THE CHER SHOW**), but the veteran Broadway cast was talented and up for the challenge, led by Terrance Mann and they made those famous songs sound great. The band was awesome. I loved watching "Watching the Wheels Go By" as four cast members sat at the lip of the stage and sang with heartfelt voices.

Yoko Ono came often to the show, and on my late shifts I would have to stand near her orchestra seat at intermission (along with her personal security) and ask that people not bother her. That included me. As instructed, I was not to speak to her either. Ushers should be seen but not heard.

My most recent venture back to the Broadhurst was to work two performances of the musical, **ANASTASIA**—I'd asked to work there, I wanted to see the show. Pretty to look at, yet uncertain whether it wanted to be either a drama or a cartoon. But I love Ahrens and Flaherty's music, and there's nothing like hearing one of their scores with a live orchestra. I was glad to help secure seats to the show for my college friend Mary's daughters, who took the bus up from their home in Virginia. They'd never been to New York. "Uncle Joe" to the rescue!

To close, here's a fun fact about the Broadhurst. In 1944, a production of Agatha Christie's **TEN LITTLE INDIANS** played this venue. It's more famously known by its American title, **AND THEN THERE WERE NONE**. Christie and I enjoyed a renaissance during the pandemic, me re-reading over 40 of her books, many of which I remembered reading when I was a teenager. But learning about that show's history was an interesting tidbit as I developed this particular diary. Dame Agatha and I were born two days apart, albeit years apart, too. The connection between my publishing life and theatre life continued to converge.

Whodunnit? Here's a clue. Usher Joe did it with the flashlight in the theatre.

DIARY EIGHTEEN

## We Live on Avenue B

Last chapter we were on West 44th Street, so now let's head one block north to West 45th Street, to the Golden Theatre. Originally named the Theatre Masque, it opened in 1927, and was renamed the John Golden after its namesake bought the building. Now owned by the Shubert Organization, and at 805 seats, it's the company's second smallest Broadway house and much desired for plays.

The Golden is one of my favorite houses to revisit, and I have done so on numerous occasions, as both usher and ticket taker. Located at the end of 45th Street toward Eighth Avenue, what I love most about the theatre is its proximity to the other theatres on the block—most nights when you arrived for your shift, you would see dozens of staff and friends from the Booth, the Schoenfeld, the Jacobs, the Music Box, and the Imperial; a nice way to say hi and get a quick catch-up on life on and gossip beyond the aisles.

I first came to the Golden in 1992 to work a ground-breaking show called **FALSETTOS**. It was actually two shows in one, originally produced off-Broadway, part of the "Marvin Trilogy," which began with **IN TROUSERS**. But the two follow-ups encompassed this show. **MARCH OF THE FALSETTOS** and **FALSETTOLAND** were set in New York City in the 80s, and they were powerful pieces about the AIDS crisis, centering on one family dealing with life, coming out, divorce, kids, love, death, and redemption. With a beautiful score by William Finn, the show was a critical hit and won Tony Awards for its book and score but missed out on the big prize. (**CRAZY FOR YOU**, the "New Gershwin Musical" won Best Musical that year). But **FALSETTOS** didn't falter, continuing to bring in the crowds; I mostly worked the side aisle in the orchestra after having started in the mezzanine. At only nine ushers (including the chief), it was an intimate experience in an intimate theatre, and I was very happy working there.

Until one night. Our regular chief was out, a substitute manager on duty as well, and the directress, the number two usher, (also the chief's daughter) was in charge. With so many sub ushers assigned to the theatre that night, it should have fallen to me to be placed in the role of director. Seniority works that way. Except I was passed up, the slot given to a substitute who was filling in for just that one night. Me being me, I questioned the choice. The sub chief's response? An F-bomb launched at me. I reported her to the office that Monday, and next thing I know...I'm transferred. But it was a good thing to remove me from a toxic person. I was much happier for the change.

Still, not my favorite memory of the Golden Theatre and one of the only negative stories I'll tell in this memoir. I like being a positive person, celebrating all that I've had the privilege to see and work and experience, and I couldn't be more grateful to the Theater Operations department at Shubert during that era.

That next week the office assigned me to work at the Imperial Theatre, then sent me back for a few more weeks. I loved the chief, Fran, one of the nicest ladies I'd met on Broadway. No F-bombs there! She kept me near her, having me work the first aisle on the orchestra level. Not a bad gig, getting to see **LES MISERABLES** nightly. It remains one of my favorite shows—top five.

March arrived and I was given a new, permanent usher slot at the Barrymore Theatre on West 47th Street. But I had worked 10 months at **FALSETTOS** and what that show did for me was make me delve into my inner self. A story of a man struggling with his sexuality, because that's what I was doing at the same time. Our stories were different, but our goal was the same, to be honest with oneself and happy. I recall one night a family of four, mom, dad, two young kids, left during the first act, clearly not pleased with the subject matter. It kind of hit me. I could never be that close-minded to the possibilities that existed in the world, or within myself. I learned a lot about myself, sometimes left in tears during the final song.

I would return to the Golden over the years when I had the chance, usually when whatever theatre I was working was dark; or maybe it was just picking up an extra show on a day off. Over the years I would see Glenn Close and John Lithgow in **A DELICATE BALANCE** (misguided revival), Carey Mulligan and Billy Nye in **SKYLIGHT** (she had to make spaghetti every night on that stage), Bill Pullman and Julia Stiles in **OLEANNA**, Zoe Caldwell and Audra McDonald in **MASTER CLASS**, Elaine May in **THE WAVERLY GALLERY** (where every week there was a different cover photo for the *Playbill*), James Earl Jones and Cicely Tyson in **THE GIN GAME**, among many others.

Then there was the hysterical **VANYA AND SONIA AND MASHA AND SPIKE** with Sigourney Weaver and David Hyde Pierce. Here was a play I could watch nightly, with clever, pithy dialogue, over-the-top performances, and great laughs. David was especially sweet—on that first preview he came to the back of the house prior to curtain and introduced himself to all the ushers. "I'm David," he said. Yeah, I knew. I was a huge "Frasier" fan. True class lives within that man. I remember our producer Joey (whom I'd worked with before) being so welcoming to me, shaking my hand and saying he was happy to have me working there. But I only lasted three weeks before the Shubert office called and offered me a promotion, the ticket taker position at the Lyceum Theatre, which was scheduled to begin previews in two days. Short notice! But I still got to attend **VANYA'S** opening night party.

What was my favorite show to play the Golden? That's easy. It's the longest-running show in their history, the funny and sometimes raunchy but always clever **AVENUE Q**. I had two different runs there over its long tenure, filled with lots of fun memories. What's interesting about that show is, as I write this, doing research to read further about the Golden's history, of previous shows. The first production to play there was called, ironically, **PUPPETS OF PASSION**. I'm sure Trekkie Monster had a good laugh about that. Although Kate Monster might be more apt given her antics during the show.

But the most memorable moment of **AVENUE Q** was the closing, a Sunday night. After a healthy five-year run, I guess either ticket sales had flattened or the Shuberts had other plans for that theatre. Q had to close, or, as we discovered during the curtain call, transfer. The producer, Kevin McCullum, came on stage and announced, just as the cast had taken their final bows, that **AVENUE Q** was moving to the off-Broadway venue New World Stages in a month's time. It kind of stole the thunder of the Broadway cast's closing because it wasn't guaranteed that THEY were transferring. The economics of off-Broadway are way different.

At the closing night party later that night, I remember having an intriguing chat with one of the cast members (they were always so nice and welcoming to the front of house staff, just one big family at the Golden), but she lamented how her closing "had been stolen" with the surprise announcement. Still, all those cast members, both humans and puppets, should be proud of all their achievements. Hell, they even managed to nab the Best Musical Tony Award away from that blockbuster up at the Gershwin on $50^{th}$ Street, **WICKED**—I'm sure they were green with jealousy. I always like when the underdogs triumph.

**WICKED** is still playing.

The Golden Theatre holds a special place in my Broadway heart, but not just because of the shows I witnessed there. It was the staff (with one f-ing notable exception). Ms. Jones, Helen, Mae, Pat, Raymond, and the entire gang at that theatre always welcomed me back. I even named a character in my Jimmy McSwain series after a sweetheart of a lady with the last name of Byrne, using it as Jimmy's mother's maiden name. Influence is everywhere.

And memories like these are, well, golden.

DIARY NINETEEN

# Broadway, 2021

Here's a change of pace. This entry doesn't start with a show or a theatre but with a…baseball game? No, it's not those **DAMN YANKEES**. Again. The day is May 9th, 2021, a Sunday, Mother's Day in fact, and my great friend Teena and I have tickets to the Mets v Diamondbacks at Citi Field. It's my first return to some semblance of normalcy, and my first return to NYC since Broadway's shutdown.

In this day and age, there's always a wrinkle that not even an iron can smooth. Turns out, our wrinkle was a ticket issue. Seems our ticket broker oversold the game (since they could only allow, at the time, 20% capacity of the stadium). Our order was refunded, and we were, as the kids say, SOL. What to do? I'd been looking forward to returning to Manhattan for the first time in 14 months. And you know what? I went.

Here's how I knew the day would go well, despite the ticket snafu. As the NJ Transit train pulled into my stop at Aberdeen-Matawan, a familiar face greeted me. One of the conductors who I would see on a regular basis was working that 10:32 train. We fist pumped and were glad to be reunited after the long absence. He and his wife had come to see **KING KONG** at the Broadway and I was able to upgrade them to awesome seats. From Row R to Row G on the aisle.

So, I felt the Broadway I knew and missed was inching ever closer to me. Not to mention the week's announcement from then-Governor Cuomo that Broadway shows could resume, at full capacity (take that Mets!) on Sept 14$^{th}$. Many shows had announced their return dates. But my return date to the city was that Sunday, and as the train passed each familiar station along the North Jersey Coast Line, I thought and reminisced about my three years of taking this train to work, the feeling both surreal and comforting.

But I was not going to work. Heck, I wasn't even going to a baseball game. Yet these two divergent worlds kept colliding all day.

As I departed the train at Penn Station, I wondered: did I still have that fast NYC walk I'm known for? Easy answer: yes. But as I walked up Eighth Avenue, I found myself darting around people out of a sense of caution. Some wore masks, some had them over their ears but under their chin, and many were just mask-less. It was like 2019 and 2021 all combined in some existential facemask experiment. What year is this? What world is this?

I tried to assess how the city felt, absorb its vibe. It was quiet, like a cell phone that hadn't been recharged.

A sadness pervaded the air, even while people tried to act normal. I met Teena and we raised a pint and ate some Buffalo wings (not perfect, I'm quite particular about my Buffalo wings), but a good reminder that we were all moving forward. The new phrase is not what you do, but whether you're fully vaccinated. I was then, and as of this writing, still.

Next stop the Playwright Celtic Pub, one of my favorite Broadway haunts. The manager recognized me (which after 14 months is maybe not a good thing, haha), but he was friendly and welcoming and Teena and I began to watch the game there. Mets up, 2-0. deGrom on the mound. It would have been fun to be there in the stands.

But back to Broadway. As we walked up Eighth, I took some pictures of darkened theatres. The Majestic had a lot of scaffolding, like the Phantom himself was getting a new mask; or maybe they were installing a new chandelier? They were scheduled to be back in October 2021 to continue their streak as the longest-running show in Broadway history. I played the score later that week. It's majestic, too.

Over on 45$^{th}$ Street, I saw familiar marquees like **AIN'T TOO PROUD** at the Imperial, **COME FROM AWAY** at the Schoenfeld, but also new signage at the Golden for a show called **THOUGHTS ON A COLORED MAN**. On 47$^{th}$ Street, the marquee at the Barrymore still displayed **THE INHERITANCE**, which wouldn't return after ending its run a week earlier than scheduled. Over at the Brooks Atkinson across the street, **SIX** would return after having its opening night shut down on the actual day of our shutdown, March 12. At the Winter Garden, **THE MUSIC MAN**, well, that looked more than ready to play its 76 trombones with its huge marquee promoting stars Hugh Jackman and Sutton Foster.

Seeing these theatres again, in person, it was like watching past and future ghosts roaming the streets, looking for their audience, seeking the applause that ends our nights.

We closed out our day on 54$^{th}$ Street, across the street from Studio 54, its marquee for the upcoming revival of **CAROLINE OR CHANGE** visible from our seats inside the restaurant. The Mets game was on in the background. Teena and I indulged, celebrated my return to Manhattan (she lives there, like I once did), with Caesar salad, lobster ravioli, creamed spinach and mashed potatoes… oh, and a delicious filet mignon. A nice, indulgent way to return to the city I adore, and a neighborhood I so love.

In the end, I knew Broadway's lights would shine again, it would just take a bit longer than expected. And hey, the Mets won (they almost never do when I'm at the game, so you're welcome). They swept a weekend series from Arizona. Proof positive miracles happen. Oh, and the Yankees won, too. **DAMN YANKEES**! Yup, Broadway is never far away and always a home run for me.

## DIARY TWENTY

# I Give My Regards, Sir Harrison

I've covered so many theatres and chronicled various experiences at them. Some theatres I just got assigned to more often than others and that's why their names appear more frequently, and one that falls in the lesser category can be found on West 49th Street. The Ambassador Theatre.

Not the most desired of houses from all I've seen, the Ambassador has an odd history. Built in 1915, its shape is less traditional than most other proscenium theatres. It has more of an oval shape, like a more compact version of the Winter Garden. It has no lower lobby or lounge, little room for facilities on the mezzanine level, and the ushers room? Well, it's a closet under a staircase that Harry Potter would find confining.

I was first supposed to work there for a show called **THE CIRCLE**, which I documented in an earlier diary. Rex Harrison's final Broadway appearance, and while I would have loved to have grown accustomed to his face, the assignment occurred on my moving into Manhattan and I had to give the shift back. It would be years before I'd grace the Ambassador's aisles.

After that, the Ambassador, even when booked, was never on my radar. Sure, they brought in the noise, brought in the funk, Charlie Brown was told he was a good man, even though his sister Sally walked away with the show (winning Kristen Chenoweth a Tony!). It would house **FOOL MOON,** a mime show where a patron insisted on renting one of the listening devices.

The first show I worked at the Ambassador, for one night only (though I think it was a Wednesday matinee) was a revival of Ibsen's **HEDDA GABLER,** starring Kate Burton in an acclaimed performance. She was amazing. But it would be a while before I'd return to 49th Street.

I was asked to work a special benefit performance of Stephen Sondheim's **PASSION,** a ten-year anniversary production that starred Michael Cerveris and Donna Murphy, recreating her Tony-winning performance. Another oddity was a special morning shift, not a show but a press event. Apple had rented out the Ambassador for the public launch on its latest product. It was a tablet, something called an iPad. So, I got to see Steve Jobs in his Broadway debut. He didn't win a Tony. He got a lot of money, though.

It's funny to think back on that now, since in my current job on Broadway I work with a tablet. That day at the Ambassador was the launch of a new technological era that continues to define our everyday lives.

And then we come to the Ambassador's biggest, longest running, and unstoppable tour de force: Kander & Ebb's fabled **CHICAGO**. I detailed a little bit of this in my Shubert Theatre diary, but the show has much more history than I previously indicated. This staged concert version was first produced at City Center by its Encores! program. People who saw it, both audience and producers, were seduced by that score and its brilliant, slimmed-down staging by director Walter Bobbie. But could this work on Broadway and a be a hit? Who would pay Broadway prices for a concert?

Yeah, turned out they would. **CHICAGO** redefined the word hit. The Encore's! production transferred first to the Richard Rodgers Theatre on West 46$^{th}$ Street, where it ran for only four months. The theatre was already booked for another Kander & Ebb show, the new musical **STEEL PIER**. So it moved to the Shubert, where it ran for six years. But the Shubert is one of the larger houses and perhaps the show couldn't sustain the costs of a dwindling audience in such a big house. **CHICAGO** was on the move again, almost like the Windy City itself was blowing the show further uptown.

In 2003, **CHICAGO** took up residence at the Ambassador Theatre, and it was the perfect melding of show and venue. It celebrated its 25$^{th}$ anniversary of playing Broadway in 2021, and now holds the distinction of being the longest-running American musical in Broadway history.

I worked at **CHICAGO** often, sometimes for a week, sometimes for a month or two. My favorite part of the show is watching that orchestra, visible on stage, and how it's incorporated into the action taking place between Roxie, Velma, Billy, Amos, Mama Morton and the rest of the cast. Even the conductor gets some lines! That music is phenomenal, played with passion and gusto by talented musicians. My favorite part? The Entr'Acte.

One year I couldn't get home for Thanksgiving, **CHICAGO** had a performance that night and they needed ushers to fill in. My friend Kevin had accepted a shift, so I took another of the available slots too. Kevin and I had a turkey dinner at a local diner on 9$^{\text{th}}$ Avenue, complete with all the trimmings and all that jazz. Then we went to work our shift.

**CHICAGO** relies a lot on foreign tourists, much like **CATS** did toward the end of its run. It's fun, entertaining, and if you don't fully grasp the irony of its story, the talent up on that stage more than makes up for it. Celebrity casting has also kept the show going, but I still think back to that original revival cast, and of course know of the show's storied history from when it first hit Broadway in the 1970s.

It had a decent run in 1975, 993 performances, but it was so ahead of its time with its scathing commentary on law and order and punishment and couldn't compete well-enough with the juggernaut that ended up saving the industry and revitalizing Times Square. Yup, **CHICAGO** lost the Best Musical Tony to **A CHORUS LINE**. But like Roxie, the show got its revenge, ("it had it coming") taking home the Best Musical Revival Tony—ironically playing at the Shubert, once home to…uh, **A CHORUS LINE**. Broadway is a long street, and it has a long memory.

**CHICAGO** is infamous for its irony.

DIARY TWENTY-ONE

## The Royale Family

I've often found myself back on 45<sup>th</sup> Street, so now let's discuss the theatre I know as both the Royale and now the Bernard B. Jacobs. It was once owned by John Golden and was briefly known as that before he moved next door to his smaller venue.

I first worked the Royale Theatre, as it was known then, in 1992 for a performance of Herb Gardner's Pulitzer nominee, **CONVERSATIONS WITH MY FATHER**, starring a Tony-winning turn by Judd Hirsch. The head usher, Helen, was a feisty, red-headed sweetheart of a lady, a bit of a flirt, but it was all done in good fun. We would ride home on the 6 train sometimes after a Sunday matinee. Whenever the Royale had a new show come in, I'd be able to secure a sub shift to see the production.

I think of **AN INSPECTOR CALLS**, an atmospheric British thriller with a cool set and rain that fell down on the company; of **COPENHAGEN**, kinda boring and long and I had to sit in the wings for the whole (did I mention it was long) show; **ANNA IN THE TROPICS**, with Jimmy

Smits and Priscilla Lopez; **ART**, a big hit for that theatre, winning the Tony for Best Play—I actually worked that one several times, with its ever-evolving cast changes. I believe I saw George Wendt (Norm!), Wayne Knight (Hello, Newman), and George Segal (Jack Gallo!). Yeah, I like my sitcoms.

In addition to working the Royale, I was able to see as a patron some interesting shows: **TRIUMPH OF LOVE**, with Betty Buckley is a highlight. But the Royale was renamed in 2005 after the famed Shubert president who had helped rebuild Broadway in the 70s and 80s. The renaming was done posthumously, but the tradition of hits at the now-Jacobs never diminished.

One of its early hits under its new marquee was **MARTIN SHORT: FAME BECOMES ME**. Now, I happen to think Martin Short is the funniest man on the planet and to sit and watch his one-man show (with four other actors) represents one of my biggest thrills of being inside that 1,078-seat theatre. I remember going to this show for another reason, it was my first official date with Eduardo. (More on him another time, sorry Steve.) But Martin Short had me laughing so hard at the start of the show when he announced, in that silly voice of his, "Thank you Bernard B. Jacobs for your theatre… whoever you are."

I also worked **ONCE**, the Tony-award winning musical (I worked it twice, haha). I was offered by head usher John, a great pal, to work it every Wednesday matinee since the other show I was working full-time didn't have Wednesday matinees, but I'd already accepted the same offer from another theatre. But we would work together again. I'm always finding myself back at the Jacobs.

I ushered the revival of **THE COLOR PURPLE** with Cynthia Erivo and Jennifer Hudson during a holiday week when most shows had different schedules, **GOD OF CARNAGE**, another big hit with James Gandolfini. **IT'S ONLY A PLAY** with Nathan Lane (we meet again) had transferred from the neighboring Schoenfeld, **'NIGHT MOTHER** with Edie Falco, Harold Pinter's **BETRAYAL**, which wasn't to my liking; **BANDSTAND**, which I didn't take to at first, but I do enjoy the cast recording. I just thought the creators told the story from the wrong point of view.

Still, the Jacobs always seems to get great bookings, and I'm thankful that I'm always welcomed back to see the show, work the house, be part of its history. But I've got one last story about the Jacobs, for now. I was asked by the Shubert office to be the second ticket taker at Opening Night of the acclaimed Irish play **THE FERRYMAN**. I'd already ushered it, and it was long! As I arrived to prepare for the night, the house manager couldn't have been less welcoming. She was handing out gifts from the producers to the staff and said to me, "I don't have one for you, Joe." I hadn't even asked for one, I was there to work. I love working openings and was happy to be part of the festivities, gift notwithstanding. Next time, just say thanks for helping out.

I would eventually become a ticket taker at the Jacobs (different manager, yay!) for the limited engagement of the classic Eugene O'Neill play **THE ICEMAN COMETH**, starring Denzel Washington. (4 hours in length!) Denzel didn't arrive on stage until nearly an hour in. Lucky him. But Denzel gets his own entry later in this memoir. Still, I'll give a sneak peek—his arrival on stage was always met with excitement and applause from the audience. He would come down one of the orchestra center aisles, giving his audience what they'd bought tickets for. It was the third show he'd starred in that I'd worked.

So, that ends a tale of one theatre, two names, many shows, and a place I always look back on fondly. I've worked every aisle, orchestra and mezzanine, the front door, and that one time, backstage for what might have been a good nap. No matter the name blazing on the marquee, this theatre will always have a royal feel to it.

DIARY TWENTY-TWO

# Four Tonys and a Funeral

Did you know I've worked the Belasco Theatre? Haha, worst-kept secret. As we near the halfway point of my stories, I think it's time to write another sub-edition of what should be called "The Belasco Diaries." This one has an empowering angle, a triumphant one, and a tragic ending, but it's all wrapped up in a production that encompassed each of those ideals.

Shall we enter **A DOLL'S HOUSE**? Henrik Ibsen's difficult, thrilling, and shattering play of a fractured marriage, a lie, featuring one of the most stellar performances I've ever seen in my 30 years on Broadway. And I got to work it for the entire six-month run.

Let's back up a bit. As the Belasco was not booked often, and when it was, sometimes the show was limited, whether intentional or…not. But I liked to keep working, so I'd made the rounds round the 'hood. From the Golden to the Barrymore, I rarely lacked for a place to call home. But in 1997, a British transfer of **A DOLL'S HOUSE** was coming to the Belasco and the office asked if I would return "home" to work that run. It was going to be a big hit, and all predictions proved correct, it was the biggest hit the Belasco had seen in years.

This was the pre-renovation version of the venerated theatre, so it still had its challenges: the separate balcony entrance foremost in my mind and I was thinking I'd be sent back upstairs, just like when I first arrived there seven years earlier. Nope, I got assigned to one of the center orchestra aisles, what we call aisle three located on house right. High profile, high volume, and as it turned out, lots of exposure to celebrities who were clamoring to come see this acclaimed show.

Now, near the aisle where I worked were the exit doors hidden behind, at the time, thick curtains. They helped block out the sounds of the traffic on 44th Street. Four sets of doors, but at the last one there was no step, so it served as our accessible entrance as well as an exit. That detail will play into my story toward the end of this entry.

Back to the show. Starring British actress Janet McTeer and Irish actor Owen Teale, both making their Broadway debuts, they led a small cast in a near-three-hour production. We began previews in March, opened on April 2nd, 1997, to thunderous reviews, claiming it was the show of the season. We were sold out every performance, eight shows a week, and my partner on the aisle, Meaghan, and I worked our tails off getting everyone seated during the 30-minute rush we call walk-in.

Before the house opened, she would serenade me with her sonorous voice, sometimes opera, an while I knew she was kidding around I thought it was an impressive sound for a young woman. She also made me laugh with her tough girl, Hell's Kitchen persona.

I remember nights when the manager would give the staff a heads-up about an important guest coming to see the show. At the time those included the likes of hot 90s celebs Julia Roberts, Keanu Reeves, and Tom Cruise, on separate nights yes, but you get the idea. This was a massive, and rare, hit for the Belasco. I remember Ms. Roberts arrived late and she had to wait for the late-seat cue for me to bring her to her seat.

**A DOLL'S HOUSE** received 4 Tony award nominations that May: Best Actress and Best Supporting Actor, Best Director, and Best Revival of a Play. The show swept their respective categories, taking home those treasured Tonys. I've worked shows with many more nominations that leave empty-handed, so this is the triumph I referenced earlier.

Originally scheduled to close the weekend of July 4th, because of the Tony sweep the show was extended until the end of August, which was great—hey, it kept us all employed that much longer. Needing a break from working two jobs, though, I took one week off and flew to Bermuda for some fun, sun, and writing. Clearing my mind. But I returned, tan and rested, ready for the final six weeks of the run, including that last, unforgettable weekend.

**A DOLL'S HOUSE** played its final performance on Sunday, August 31st, an evening show which I believe was a benefit for the Actor's Fund. There were rumblings throughout the house that a special guest was coming that night, and that's where the accessible entrance came in handy. It was Christopher Reeve, Superman himself, in a big wheelchair and equipped with his breathing apparatus which made hissing sounds throughout the show. Witnessing his inner strength, able to see his wide, knowing eyes, he was empowering and inspiring.

Okay, here's where the story takes its tragic turn. I was on the late shift that night and the streets of Manhattan were quiet after eleven o'clock. Sunday night of a holiday weekend. As I was walking across Madison Avenue at 44th Street, I noticed the M1 bus was a block away, so instead of going to the 4, 5, 6 subway at Grand Central I hopped the arriving bus, as I often did. The bus driver zoomed up the avenue, the lights synchronized, so we barely stopped—all we could see was a sea of green orbs as we journeyed north. I felt a bit nervous, though. With so few people on the bus, which meant fewer stops, I knew I'd be home faster than a normal bus ride home. In my mind, though, I was signaling to the driver: "slow down." I was quickly let out at 89th Street and walked the rest of the way home to 311 east of 2nd Avenue.

That's when I heard the news of Princess Diana's car accident and eventual passing.

**A DOLL'S HOUSE** is the story of a marriage broken by lies, of fractured relationships, and ultimately the decision to take control of your life on your own terms. Ibsen wrote his play in 1879. Huh. So many memories arise from that run, such impactful moments of my life interspersed with reality, with truth, bits of history caught up in the final clack of Nora closing the door on her former life.

DIARY TWENTY-TWO

# The Litter Box

Okay, that was heavy, so let's lighten things here with a visit to, well, the Heaviside Layer. Here's the now and forever story of the times I've worked one of the most iconic theatres on Broadway. From Jellicle cats to Dancing Queens on a Greek Island, then a prize fight in the form of a musical, this is the Winter Garden Theatre. Well, Part One at least.

I remember when I was first interviewing for publishing jobs in New York City, one of my appointments was located on a top floor at 1633 Broadway, at 50$^{th}$ Street. Across the street a huge marquee and even bigger poster advertised for something called **CATS**. While I didn't get the job then at 1633 (I'd work for that company later, when they moved to 375 Hudson Street), I would eventually land a shift beneath that marquee.

Here's how that first shift happened. I hadn't yet been officially hired by The Shubert Organization, but when you're in the union technically you can work for any of the organizations. It all about connections. One late Friday afternoon I called the union office for work, and they said they had a last-minute need at the Winter Garden, a slot the Shubert office couldn't fill for whatever reason. It was my first-ever Shubert-owned theatre I worked at. I knew none of the staff, and they didn't know me.

Let's say I went through a hazing process. Not intentional, but still, it was memorable.

The Winter Garden has a complicated seating plan, less traditional than most of the other theatres. There I am, trying to learn the layout, there were numerous inserts to put into the *Playbill*s, all to be done within 30 minutes, and I also had to change into my usher clothes, all done before we opened the house at 7:30. I was anxious to prove myself, of course.

Prior to the end of the first act, I was informed by the head usher that I was to sit on the "tire," my job to prevent patrons from walking up on the stage with drinks. But here's the twist. There were two tires! The tradition at **CATS** was that the character of Old Deuteronomy would sit on the big tire on stage during intermission, greeting patrons who could go up on the stage at that interval. But I'd been told to go there, too. I walked up the ramp and approached the big tire, where the actor playing OD gave me a strange look. Kind of like, "what are you doing?" Not unlike how any actual cat would act!

One of the regular ushers came running toward me and directed me to the lip of the stage between the two ramps, where, amidst the other junk that decorated the set, was a shard of a rubber tire. That's where I was supposed to sit. Would have been nice to have that info in advance! But there I sat, a bright light from the mezzanine blazing in my eyes, as I tried to discourage people with drinks to not come onto the stage.

Not sure of the timeline as it relates to this story, but I'm leaving my apartment building on 90$^{th}$ Street, and I see one of my neighbors wearing a **CATS** show jacket. I asked him if he was in the show, and indeed he was. Part of the chorus, and he also understudied OD. Thankfully he wasn't on that night of the tire incident. But what our encounter led to was an ongoing friendship with a neighbor in a Manhattan walk-up, not something that normally occurs in this city. Thanks, Jay.

I would work the show many times more, and even got to see Jay go on as OD. I stuffed his insert into the *Playbill* and thought what a coincidence, neighbors on both sides of the stage. Then I watched him—heard him. What a voice, deep, almost operatic.

**CATS** was never a favorite to work for our ushering gang. After playing Broadway for so many years—18 years in total —it had taken its critical hits from the locals. But the tourists loved it, and it was them who kept the show running for all those years. When Grizabella the Glamour Cat would sing "Memory" toward the end of the show you could hear the silence fall upon the audience; because this was the moment they were waiting for.

One week, while my regular theatre was closed, I needed to seek sub work elsewhere. Usually that would entail calling the office for work on Monday morning, but the Friday before I realized Monday was a holiday and the office would be closed. So, I quickly called Mary, and was told by her, "I only have a week at the Winter Garden." If I wanted to work that next week, I had no choice but to accept. I replied, "I guess it's my turn." Talk about a memory!

Look, **CATS** gave Broadway a huge boost, ran for 18 years. With its 1,526-seat capacity, it must have resonated with many people. I like certain parts of the score, including the one song that didn't make it onto the original cast recording, "The Awful Battle of the Peaks and the Pollicles." I take exception to that song's exclusion, yeah, I knew it was a show about cats, but this song was about dogs. Shadow agrees with me.

What I will say about the Winter Garden during those feline days was how nice the staff was to me, despite that first day tire-mishap. As a newbie, I was initiated into the litter, given decent breaks that were like catnip, and when the show was over, I'd go home and yawn a big meow. Because Jellicles can and Jellicles do.

I promised more about the Winter Garden. Part 2 (boop) begins after the turn of the page. Gonna Fly Now.

DIARY TWENTY-FOUR

## In This Corner...Fernando

Well, here we go again. Still on 50$^{th}$ and Broadway at the Winter Garden Theatre, now beautifully restored after ascending to the Heaviside Layer for all those years. Now, it's time to travel to a Greek Island, so take a chance on me as we start this entry with...**MAMMA MIA**.

I'd seen the show in London (except the night I had a ticket to the Prince Edward Theatre its lobby flooded; I had to come back the next night), but I hadn't yet been to see the Broadway version. **MAMMA MIA** was the first show to open on Broadway after 9/11, in October of 2001, and the reviews were beyond great. It was just the happy, feel-good tonic New York City—and the country—needed at the time. Turns out, a few years later, it was just what I needed.

I'd been away from the Shubert Organization for two years, working at the independent Circle in the Square Theatre; it's schedule and run-time worked with the rest of my life. But the show I had been ushering, **THE 25$^{TH}$ ANNUAL PUTNAM COUNTY SPELLING BEE**, was closing at the end of January after a two-and-a-half-year successful run. The publishing company I was working for was in the process of downsizing, and I fell victim to that "elimination of my job." I left that job on a Friday, and that same weekend worked the final four performances of **SPELLING BEE**. By Sunday night, I was suddenly out of two jobs.

New York State Department of Labor was of no help. See, I also write books and the woman at unemployment denied my claim because I'd just published a book (to small sales, sorry to say). "Are you the author of 'London Frog'?" she asked, and when I acknowledged that I was, she informed me I had to record each day I wrote my new book as a day of work—despite the fact I had no new contract. I'd been Googled by NYS Labor!

Enter the Shubert's again. I called the office and after getting through the "Where have you been" question, I was given a Wednesday matinee shift that week at the Winter Garden. It was February and winter often offers up discontent in terms of available work. After I seated the people for the 2:00 pm show, I was taking my break in front of the theatre and wondering how I'd come so far, but how I'd found my life slipping through my fingers. It was a depressing day, like I'd lost what I'd worked so hard for. Things would improve, though, that story for another time.

Let's stay with the Winter Garden, and a better experience that happened years later. It was the most unlikely idea for a stage musical, one based on a famous movie with a famous song and some famous sequels with another equally famous song. We're talking **ROCKY**.

They didn't call it **ROCKY: THE MUSICAL**, just **ROCKY** Broadway. It seemed an odd marketing decision to me. If you're putting on a show, let the audience know what they're getting. Yup, Rocky sings. Punchlines were the order of the day when the show was announced. But you know what, I liked the show a lot, and I had a blast working the front doors for a few weeks during early previews, which culminated in being invited back to work in opening night.

What happened was this: one Monday morning, I got a call from the house manager at the Winter Garden, informing me they were in need of a ticket taker for a few weeks, as one of the two regulars wasn't coming back immediately. I was between shows at the Belasco, so I readily accepted. **ROCKY** had its issues, but also its strengths, and I'm a sucker for the scores of Ahrens and Flaherty. Even though this wasn't their best, it still had some beautiful melodies.

But the attraction was the set—just how were they going to pull off the running up the steps of the Philadelphia Art Museum, the slaughterhouse where he punches large pieces of animal flesh, and finally, the prize fight with Apollo Creed at the end. Well, they did it, but not without its technical complications. I remember one Friday night during Act I the set broke down—not the boxing ring, we weren't up to that point. Stage management had to stop the show. It was going to be a while the manager informed the staff, and then came an announcement over the PA system informing patrons of the delays and that they were being treated to a drink at the bar, courtesy of the show. Thanks, Sly.

Problem was, they hadn't informed the bar staff in advance of the coming onslaught. But the bartenders rallied and did their jobs and kept pouring those drinks. Kudos to the gang at Theatre Refreshment! The set would break down a couple more times during previews, but the stagehands and creative staff worked out the kinks during the preview period.

The most thrilling part of **ROCKY** was the climax, the fight, when the boxing ring was extended over the first eight rows of the orchestra. The orchestra ushers would have to organize the patrons from their ticketed seats and onto bleachers on the stage, clearing those rows for the hydraulics that pushed the boxing ring ever closer for more effective viewing for the entire audience. One night, a patron refused to get up from her "great seat," and the usher stated if she remained in her seat her head would be cut off. She got up.

My last shift at **ROCKY** was opening night, where I got to work the third door, that night the VIP door. I scanned the tickets for Sylvester Stallone and his family, among others. Then it was on to the opening night party at Roseland on 52$^{nd}$ Street, and it, of course, featured a boxing ring that attendees could go into. My guest that night was my now ex, Eduardo. We donned shiny robes, blue and red, put on the gloves, and danced around the ring like true competitors. It was a memorable night. I remember the food, too, lots of Philly snacks like cheese steak sliders.

But this is a story of the Winter Garden Theatre. **MAMMA MIA** would be moved to the Broadhurst, and **ROCKY** didn't last too long, only a few months. Next show I worked, just once, was the successful **SCHOOL OF ROCK**, another Wednesday matinee and seating school groups. But the Winter Garden always rises again and is never long for a booking. As of this writing, **THE MUSIC MAN** with Hugh Jackman and Sutton Foster is dancing and singing up big receipts!

DIARY TWENTY-FIVE

# The Great Hair-Flip of 1997

Even with my publishing career gaining me accolades and promotions, I still couldn't give up my theatre job. It's the late '90s and between the two jobs it's almost like I'm living a Jekyll & Hyde kind of life. Wait, wasn't there a musical on Broadway around that time? Sure was, and I worked it for the bulk of its run at the Plymouth Theatre on 45th Street.

I was already familiar with **JEKYLL & HYDE**, having bought the original concept album (on cassette, no less!), featuring Colm Wilkinson, whom I knew from **LES MIZ**, and Linda Eder, a singer I wasn't previously familiar with. Well, that was all about to change. A few years later, the composer and co-creator of the show, Frank Wildhorn, released a double-CD featuring the complete, intended score of J&H, subtitled The Gothic Musical Thriller. I bought that one, too. This time we had Australian actor and singer Anthony Warlowe playing the lead dual roles and as Lucy...well, Linda Eder was back. Turned out, at the time, she was not just Wildhorn's muse but his eventual wife.

When J&H was announced for Broadway, I was working over at the Belasco, but I wanted to finally see live on stage this show I'd heard so often on my CD player. I actually bought tickets, went with my friend Mike, I believe during the July 4th weekend of 1997. Sitting in the first row of the mezzanine, I thought with anticipation, "This is the Moment!" (For those not in the know, that was the title of the biggest song from the show! And had been played in many other venues, including figure skating during the Olympics.) But then the show started. Oh, how disappointed I was in the staging; I felt the director had held back from embracing its full pop potential, but this was an era when the epic British musicals it was trying to emulate were out of vogue. I kept wanting to like it, for it to push itself to its full potential. Then in Act II, Emma and Lucy, the two romantic leads for the drug-addled title(s) role, broke free of those confining red walls of the set and sang the roof off the Plymouth with a song called "In His Eyes." I let out a sigh of relief. I got what I'd come for.

Cut to Fall '97, the Belasco's show, a limited run featuring Mandy Patinkin in his one-man show **MAMALOSHEN** finished up, so I was asked by the head usher at the Plymouth if I wanted a four-week stint, as one of her regular ushers was going to be on a leave. I readily accepted—the Plymouth is considered a prime house on Broadway, rarely dark, and after those four weeks I was invited to join the staff full-time. I took it, and until J&H closed in January of 2001, I had steady work. That's rare in our business.

When I arrived for my new stint, some of the original cast had departed and new cast members had started —with the awesome, big-voiced Rob Evan taking on the dual role. J&H was defying the odds of success on Broadway, poorly reviewed by the critics, no Hollywood stars to help sell tickets, but what it managed to achieve was simple: it was an over-the-top crowd pleaser with a big-sounding score that helped spread word of mouth.

What also kept me happy at the Plymouth was the amazing house staff. While we had a revolving door of managers during the run (and beyond, to other shows), the bulk of the ushering staff stayed a long time. Francine, the head usher, Roz the ticket taker, and then the gang: Bobbie, Carrie, Marco, Kevin, Mark, Betty, Helen, among some others. But this was a tight group; many of us would go out for drinks after a weekend show. We even went bowling a couple of times at the lanes inside the Port Authority Bus Terminal. We laughed a lot before every show as we stuffed our *Playbill*s with far too many inserts some nights.

The producers were intent on keeping the show running, and they began to hire a series of "known" names from the mediums of TV and music to take on the roles of Jekyll and Hyde. First up was Jack Wagner, of "General Hospital" and "Melrose Place" fame. To say the suburban ladies came in droves to see him is an understatement. Who didn't want to see Frisco Jones live on stage? It was all they needed. Most weekends the seats were packed. I think he played a six-month run. Jack made some, uh, interesting acting choices, I thought. But he sure sold tickets.

Oh, and then enter the rock star: Sebastian Bach of Skid Row notoriety. What a presence, and in truth, a total good guy. He liked hanging with the staff; one of our ushers would run and get him coffee prior to the show. One of the fun things about the Plymouth back then was the front of house staff had to enter through the stage door, as opposed to being buzzed through the main doors by someone in the box office. That's how we got to know the cast, and it was one big family. At the end of each of his performances, Sebastian would take the final bow of course, and his adoring fans would toss stemmed roses up on to the stage. He'd grab one, bite the petals off and then spit them out over the crowd. They roared. Guess the word had gotten out, because the number of roses rose with each night.

I remember one Saturday night: J&H's 999th performance. There was a party planned after the show to celebrate the upcoming 1,000$^{th}$ show to be performed the next day. Cut to Sunday matinee, pieces of the skylight on the roof of the Plymouth were raining down on the stage.

The performance had to be canceled.

The Lesson here? Don't celebrate that which has not happened yet.

(Side note: the next Tuesday's performance went up, that was number 1,000.)

Our final big name to be cast in the title(s) role was none other than David Hasselhoff. He began in October of 2000, with an official opening night on Halloween, where, after the show, cast and crew and FOH were treated to a lavish party at the Russian Tea Room. Next day the reviews came out, and read into this what you may, soon thereafter up went our closing notice. January 7, 2001. The longest-running show in the history of the Plymouth, it played 1,543 performances.

We were also raising money during the Hoff's period for Broadway Cares/Equity Fights AIDS, and oh, how he loved speaking to the crowd during the curtain call address. Once the fund-raising had ended, his speech continued. His "dream of playing Broadway" like an endless loop eight times a week. Until the merciful end of his run.

But during the run of J&H, composer Frank Wildhorn achieved a feat few other Broadway composers have managed: at one point, he had three shows running on the Great White Way. **THE SCARLET PIMPERNAL** was struggling at the Minskoff and **THE CIVIL WAR** had just opened at the St. James Theatre. I think Andrew Lloyd Webber had been the most recent person to have reached such an accomplishment. What was interesting was that the three shows were playing at all three Broadway organizations. J&H was Shubert, **PIMPERNAL** was

Nederlander, and **CIVIL** was Jujamcyn. Not sure that's ever been done.

Wildhorn has his detractors, and sure, I get it, but I've always enjoyed his soaring ballads and unabashed anthems. J&H remains my favorite, with **SCARLET PIMPERNAL** a close second, but I suppose for me it's about more than the show which books the house, it's the fond memories evoked by this lovely, 1079-seat theatre. How many nights did I sit on those stairs, watching as Jekyll and his alter-ego Hyde battled each other, distinguishable only from whether his hair was in a ponytail or flaying about with the whip of his body.

Sure, the Plymouth was renamed the Gerald Schoenfeld Theatre in 2004, but for the six years I remained working there, it was always the Plymouth. It was my rock.

### DIARY TWENTY-SIX

# At Least There Was No Math

It's taken a while to circle back to 50th Street, but it's always a fun return "uptown." Let's revisit arguably Broadway's most unique and innovative theatre: Circle in the Square.

I've had several stints at Circle, as I like to abbreviate it, and I'll get to one particularly notable experience at the that house in a future entry. For now, I'm going to S-P-E-L-L out 26 reasons why I love this theatre. Was that enough of a hint? We're here to alphabetize the laughs and growing pains that was the long-running, acclaimed, Tony-winning show called **THE 25TH ANNUAL PUTNAM COUNTY SPELLING BEE**. My story is best told through, well, letters. Hang on, this will take every letter.

A: AISLES. Circle has three sets of doors in which to approach the seating area. Its unique design could place you in the odd-numbered section or the even-numbered section, divided by the 100 and 200 seat sections. For **SPELLING BEE**, Circle was set up with a horseshoe-shaped thrust stage. Patrons would be sent to Aisles 1, 2, or 3.

B: BLEACHERS. The set for the show took place in a gymnasium, where not only did the cast sit on wooden benches, so too did some of the patrons. The first couple of rows down on the orchestra floor were also benches, giving theatregoers a close-up view of the action, almost as if they were in the gym, too.

C: CEILA, as in Celia Keenan-Bolger. Tony-nominated for her role as teenager Olive Ostrovsky, her character to me was the emotional heart of the show. Innocent and vulnerable, the typical young adult searching for meaning in her life. Celia would later win a Tony Award for playing another teenager, Scout in **TO KILL A MOCKINGBIRD**.

D: DIRECTOR. We had one of the best in the business in James Lapine, who has so many Broadway credits and awards to his name throughout the years it would take beyond a "Who's Who in the Cast" paragraph in the *Playbill* to name them. He's worked with amazing composers like Stephen Sondheim and William Finn—in this case, the latter.

E: ESCALATOR. Since Circle is located underground, patrons, after having their tickets scanned, would have to ride down the escalator and then be directed to their appropriate aisle. At the end of the show, we would switch the direction of the escalator, so the people could depart the theatre. I loved when I had access to the key to do this. I felt important!

F: FINN, as in the show's composer and lyricist,

William Finn. He's best known for **FALSETTOS** and several off-Broadway incarnations of that show, as well as LCT's **A NEW BRAIN**. Finn is a deceptively talented, tuneful songwriter.

G: GAD. I'm talking the now-famous Josh Gad of Olaf infamy from **FROZEN**. He was one of the replacements for the character of William Barfee (Bar-*fay*)

H: HIT! That's what the New York Times said: "How do you spell H-I-T?" The show ran for 1,136 performances. They got that spelling right.

I: IMPROVISATION: Jay Reiss played Vice Principal Panch, and it was his job during the bee to give the spellers their word. He would use the word in oddly written sentences to help provide a definition of the word. With the guest spellers from the audience, he often had to make stuff up on the spot. Future Panch's included Darrell Hammond and Mo Rocca.

J: JESSE. The part of Leaf Coneybear was played with comic delight by a then-unknown actor named Jesse Tyler Ferguson. This show changed his life, as he would ultimately go on to Hollywood fame in the sitcom Modern Family, but also make returns to Broadway. He's proof you don't forget your theater roots.

K: KIDS. It was a great Broadway show to take kids to. Seemingly innocent in tone, but **SPELLING BEE** had an sliver's edge while also delivering a powerful message. The joy of finding other kids who enjoyed spelling emboldened a competitive spirit usually found among the jocks. Also, some of the kids attending the show got to up on stage and spell and gave them a taste of theater from the other side of the seats.

L: As in LISA. Oh, Ms. Peretti herself, the fabulous and friendly Lisa Howard. She would always come down Aisle 3 to make her entrance, holding the winner's trophy at the start of the show. She'd wave hello to the crowd, then to me and my partner on the aisle. I always said, "Hi, Ms. Peretti." Then she would take charge for the next 1:45 minutes as the soul of the show.

M: MAGIC FOOT. Barfee's way of knowing how to spell the word, he would direct his foot and glide it across the floor, imagining how to properly spell the word. Both comedic and touching.

N: NO WEDNESDAY MATINEES! We did two shows on Sunday to make up our 8-show a week schedule. That worked well with my day job, I didn't have to disappear for two hours.

O: ORIGINAL CAST: In addition to those actors mentioned elsewhere: Derrick Baskin (**MEMPHIS, AIN'T TOO PROUD**), Deborah S. Craig, co-creator Sarah Saltzberg, and Jose Llana (**ALADDIN**).

P: PRODUCERS. Many. But led by David Stone (who had a wicked big hit upstairs at the Gershwin), he led a team of dedicated professionals who kept the show running from April 15, 2005 to January 20, 2008.

Q: QUIRKY. In a musical season dominated by big hits like **MONTY PYTHON'S SPAMALOT, DIRTY ROTTEN**

SCOUNDRELS and **A LIGHT IN THE PIAZZA**, the intimate **SPELLING BEE** held its own in a very competitive season. While only one show could win the Tony for Best Musical (it went to **SPAMALOT**), all four productions enjoyed long runs, a unique year for Broadway.

R: REPLACEMENT CASTS AND UNDERSTUDIES: Barrett Foa, Stanley Bahorek, Jennifer Simard, Rory O'Malley, James Monroe Iglehart, Kate Weatherhead, just to name a bunch.

S: SUPERCALIFRAGISTICEXPIALIDOCIOUS. We had a special guest speller one night, the one, the only, the charming Julie Andrews. She was one of four audience members selected to join our spellers for one of the cleverest parts of the show. Her word? Yes, even Mary Poppins could see that coming, and—this is truth, she got it wrong and was eliminated from the bee. During the curtain call she took a bow and proved herself worthy of the **BEE**, as she proceeded to spell the word correctly — and backwards. That was an incredible night.

T: TONY AWARDS. Six nominations, two wins. One for Rachel Sheinkin for Best Book of a Musical and Dan Fogler for Best Featured Actor.

U: USHERS. What a great staff we had. Georgia, Pat (our TT), Sophie, Margie, manager Shawn, John, and the incomparable Tammy, who sadly passed the day after we closed. More on her in another entry. Also, can't forget Kelly, Allyson, Jason, Joe & Eric (who would later star in **KING KONG**!)

V: VULGAR? Wait, wasn't this show kid-friendly? Well, every once in a while we would have a designated "adult" night during our Sunday evening performances. I think we called them "Blue Nights." Kids under 16 were not admitted, and the language…well, it made for a funny night of improv. Try spelling…um, I'm not going there.

W: WRANGLERS. A team whose jobs it was to interview audience members during walk-in, attempting to sign up four people per show to join the cast on stage. Both kids and adults were chosen, though given one caveat after being chosen: NO PHOTOS ALLOWED. I confiscated my share of cameras during the run, including one matinee where the police had to be called because of a defiant parent. I let the manager handle that one.

X: Xavier, one of our ushers.

Y: YOU don't know what the show was originally called in development? C-R-E-P-U-S-C-U-L-E.

Z: SZYGY. Okay, there's a bit of a cheat here. It's the word that won Ms. Peretti the trophy back when she was in school and participating in her own spelling bee. It means, "a pair of connected or corresponding things."

Seems appropriate. Cast and crew had that and more with **SPELLING BEE**. Hope you had F-U-N with this one.

\
-

## INTERMISSION

# Remembering Sondheim

My earliest Stephen Sondheim memory is owning the 45 RPM of "Send in the Clowns," sung by Judy Collins on Elektra records. I liked that song. But I didn't know his work until years later when I bought the LP of **INTO THE WOODS**. I liked much of it, but the title track drove my roommate Mike nuts. I was just beginning to expand my musical theatre horizons beyond **A CHORUS LINE** and **PIPPIN** and **SOUTH PACIFIC**, and I knew to some Sondheim was considered a God.

I was always partial to bigger shows like **LES MIZ, PHANTOM, SAIGON**. I liked their epic sense of sung-thru storytelling, their bombast and stirring anthems. Sondheim to me remained an enigma, his melodies more complex, his lyrics…plentiful. Until one July 4th in 1990 I had an awakening.

I'd begun my ushering life a few months earlier and was steadily acquiring a CD library of famous shows. I owned a 5-disc CD carousel stereo and so that night I inserted 5 Sondheim discs. **MERRILY WE ROLL ALONG,**

**COMPANY, FOLLLIES, SUNDAY IN THE PARK WITH GEORGE** and **PACIFIC OVERTURES**. Then I hit shuffle and let the music and lyrics speak to me.

Perhaps not the best approach to learning Sondheim, because I had to keep pouring over the liner notes to know what show, what song, was playing. But I was seeking an understanding of his themes and style, studying his words and musical compositions. I spent the night playing them through.

I owned **SWEENEY TODD** on cassette (!) but had initial trouble with that show. I would invite a date to the Patti Lupone/Michael Cerveris revival at the Eugene O'Neill back in 2007 and after 15 minutes he'd ditched the show. And me. So, there's that memory. Happy Valentine's Day!

I would work **PASSION** as an usher for several months at the Plymouth. So, I grew to learn that show well and enjoyed the performances from Donna Murphy, Jere Shea and Marin Mazzie. I took my parents to see the **A FUNNY THING HAPPENED ON THE WAY TO THE FORUM** revival with Nathan Lane at the St James. I also had the privilege of seating Sondheim and scanning his ticket many times over the years. The audience always knew when he arrived. A quiet reverence would settle over the house as he took his seat.

I own all his shows now in various formats, mostly CD, and I continue to appreciate, learn, and soak in the adoration for his artistry from my Broadway friends and from Steve, a true advocate for the composer's complexity and artistry.

Here's what binds this tale of remembrance. I bought this double CD which celebrates the career of producer Cameron Mackintosh, and one of the highlights is a song called "Dueling Pianos," performed by Andrew Lloyd Webber and Stephen Sondheim sitting opposite each other at two pianos. It's a funny amalgam of "Send in the Clowns" and "Music of the Night."

What I learned from seeing that performance on a DVD and listening to it: both composers share the same birthday. I'm still learning, even after 32 years working Broadway. For my Steve's birthday in June 2020, we had tickets to the gender-bending revival of **COMPANY**. It would have been our first shared live Sondheim show. We'll get there. (And as of this writing, we did—I worked it and I got him a ticket and we got to sit together.) No need then, to send in the clowns. Don't bother—they were there.

A life beautifully lived, Mr. Sondheim. Isn't it rich?

# ACT II

## Please Take Your Seats

DIARY TWENTY-SEVEN

## One of the Great Ones

Up on 48th Street, there's a couple of theatres west of Broadway which evaded me for many years—one still does. But I'm here to talk about the one I finally discovered, and in the process, found that it was one of the great ones. Perhaps even three great ones. I'll explain. Let's get our tickets scanned and go inside the Longacre Theatre. It's a place I had almost no history with, only to see it become one of my favorite places to work.

Let's start in the distant past. The Longacre was named after Longacre Square, which was the original name for Times Square. It's 1912, and impresario Harry Frazee had built this 1,091-seat, three-level theatre. He was also known as the owner of the Boston Red Sox. A great piece of history about the Longacre, whether truth or lore, is that Frazee, to finance his stage productions, needed to raise money. What did he do? He sold the contract of one of the great ones, Babe Ruth, to the New York Yankees.

Oops. The urban myth grew from there, as the Longacre was thought as cursed as Red Sox Nation, with superstitious producers wary of booking the house—48th Street doesn't have the same foot traffic as say, 45th Street. But it's not entirely true, because over the years, while the Longacre has seen its share of flops, it's had its hits and Tony-winning performances.

It's just the flops that tended to get noticed more. **PRYMATE? THE OLDEST LIVING CONFEDERATE WIDOW TELLS ALL** (but only for one night).

When I first started ushering, I was never, by luck of the draw, sent to the Longacre. Mostly because it wasn't open much. This was the 90s, and it went through some literal dark days. They did get some notable shows though: Diana Rigg in **MEDEA** (didn't work it), Horton's Foote's **THE YOUNG MAN FROM ATLANTA** (didn't work it), Tom Selleck in **A THOUSAND CLOWNS** (didn't work it). The Longacre kept eluding me.

But they did have big hits. **AIN'T MISBEHAVIN', CHILDREN OF A LESSER GOD, A DAY IN THE LIFE OF JOE EGG, DEF POETRY JAM.**

But the Longacre was in need of a renovation, and it got one in the 2000s. A new marquee, expanded facilities, new seats, highly detailed craftsmanship on the frescoes and artwork which adorned the auditorium. While I'd seen the older version of the Longacre, I'd never worked its aisles until the restoration was complete, and when I walked in: WOW. It was beautiful. At the time I was a regular at the Belasco, pre-renovation, and I was jealous of the attention the company had given to this theatre as opposed to mine.

The first show I ever worked at the Longacre was **BOEING-BOEING**, a farce starring Mark Rylance, Christine Baranski, and Bradley Whitford. Just three performances assigned to me, a weekend pick-up. See, I'd been away at a friend's wedding (in Italy!), returning on a Friday morning. Which meant, since our weeks began on Monday or Tuesday, the office had demanded I take off the entire week from my regular assignment at the Belasco. They managed to find me work at the Longacre upon my return. And while I was happy to finally cross that theatre off my bucket list, it meant I missed the last weekend of **PASSING STRANGE** (more on that in a future diary). This is all about the Longacre.

I would sub usher various other shows at the Longacre. One of the perks of the ushering gig is that sometimes you have different schedules than other shows, so you can sneak in an extra shift. Best done during the holiday weeks. I worked **FIRST DATE** with Zachary Levi and Krista Rodriguez on a snowy December matinee; I got to see Chris O'Dowd and James Franco in **OF MICE AND MEN** on a Saturday matinee.

Then there was the devastatingly bad play **LIVING ON LOVE**, starring opera star Renee Fleming, Douglas Sills, Anna Clumsky, and Jerry O'Connell. Great cast! Terrible show. I was asked to work the mezzanine level and after the show started, I had my choice of seat. Seriously, the theatre was half-empty. But my best memory from that afternoon was at intermission, where I got to talk with Mr. O'Connell's wife and kids. Rebecca Romjin couldn't have been sweeter. I asked the kids if their dad was as silly at home as he was in the show. "Sillier." Cute kids.

But I'm saving the best for last, and here's where we get to a show that featured a true great one. **A BRONX TALE**. I was available for a few months between shows at my then-regular theatre, the Broadway, when I was asked by the head usher at the Longacre to join them. I worked the show for many months, and I loved everything about it. The staff, the show, the theatre. **A BRONX TALE** was the little show that could. No Tony nominations, but yet it holds the weekly box office record at the Longacre, nonetheless.

One of the great thrills of working this show nightly was watching how seamlessly the amazing cast worked together. You could tell they loved their show, and that translated to the audience. It was a true word of mouth show. There were no "names" in the show but being based on a play and movie written by famed actor Chazz Palminteri, **A BRONX TALE** had a built-in audience. He was frequently in attendance—he knew his audience and added to that effective word of mouth. Jersey came to Broadway!

But there was one emerging star, a guy by the name of Nick Cordero. He was already a Tony nominee for

**BULLETS OVER BROADWAY** that had played the St. James a couple years earlier. But with **A BRONX TALE,** he took command of that stage, imparting to his young protégé Calogero a simple message —that in this life, you get three great ones. His song "One of the Great Ones" was a perfect summation of the show's theme, and as it turned out, Mr. Cordero's life.

It was terrible seeing the story of Mr. Cordero's battle with Covid-19 unfold, played out on national television, and I was so sad when he passed. I thought of those nights on the aisle, seeing such talent and devotion to his craft, his joy. He was tall. It's like he stretched all the way to the balcony himself. Yeah, in 30 years of working front of the house, I'd witnessed one of the great ones.

I'll finish with this. On 48th Street, I'll take the Babe, Nick, but I need one more. How about the Longacre itself. More than a century of history lives on its stage, in its wings and its boxes and will continue to do so. **DIANA: THE MUSICAL** re-opened the Longacre after the shutdown, and while that show itself closed earlier than expected, **DIANA** was another great one ready to take on the challenge of the ghost light.

DIARY TWENTY-EIGHT

## Drink with Me

All that I can say about this entry is this: it's about time to bring him home to you little people and lovely ladies and masters of the house. As I write this on my own, I look around at the empty chairs at empty tables and wish, that at the end of the day, you'll drink with me. Let's get to the turntable, for one more day of **LES MISERABLES**.

I got a bunch of them in! Stars must be aligned.

Before I started working on Broadway, I was obsessed with the music of **LES MIZ**. I had purchased the Original London Cast recording at Tower Records in the East Village, back when such a thing existed, and listened to the double-album continually (unless I was busy playing **PHANTOM**...). I detailed in an earlier diary about the first time I saw the show at the Broadway, but this entry is all about my days after the show's transfer to the Imperial Theatre on 45th Street. I've had three separate stints, first at the original Broadway production after it had moved, and then the second revival. (I missed the first revival brought in from the road to set up a short run at the Broadhurst.)

A soaring, sweeping, epic score, a myriad of characters and plotlines, boiling down Victor Hugo's 1,000-plus page book into three-and-a-quarter hours of pure sung-through musical magic. I know the show had its critics and didn't open to overwhelming raves, but I am not among them. It is my third favorite musical of all time. (Ha, that sets up questions…which are the first two? Easy, **RAGTIME** and **CAROUSEL**). I'd never worked the Imperial prior to **LES MIZ**—but then again, I think it had always been playing there since I'd begun my ushering life.

The Imperial is, at 1,417 seats, the fourth largest of the Shubert-owned houses, and truth be told, it's not an easy house to seat. Particularly the mezzanine. While the orchestra level seating is traditional, three sections, evens and odds and consecutive 100s in the center, the mezz is another story. You need to look at the tickets very carefully. There is a front mezz, with four sections that all have the same numbers. So, you have to double-check which section your patron is in. Then there's the rear mezz, which has five sections, and many of the numbers go backwards depending on what aisle you are assigned. Have I confused you yet? I was often, but everyone got seated eventually.

Here was my method. I used to say aloud the seat location when presented with mezzanine tickets, emphasizing front or rear, and then what section. All as the sold-out crowd is pouring up the stairs, ultimately just expecting you to hand them a *Playbill*. Uh, it's not that easy and I'd like to see them master this house. (Yup, another **LES MIZ** joke.)

I would work **LES MIZ** for a three-month stretch of time after my time at **FALSETTOS** but before my run at soon-to-be reassignment to **THE SISTERS ROSENSWEIG** at the Barrymore. There were some nights the sweet head usher, Fran, would bring me down to work the orchestra level, usually the side aisle. I had to run fast to seat rows A-T, plus run up a flight of stairs to seat the three boxes. I was younger then.

But then the show would begin, and if it was my late shift, I would just watch, listen, trying not to let on to my fellow co-workers how much I loved the show. I mean, I was entitled to a break during each act, and yeah, I took them. Sometimes you needed some air outside. But I sure had my favorite moments while watching the show and I'd be sure to catch them. The thrilling first stirring notes of "At the End of the Day" still chills me. And of course, the ending number was to me, pure emotion and power. I looked forward to hearing it…feeling it…it each night. The rallying cry in the last two minutes never disappointed me as the ghosts of the cast gave soaring voice to its anthem. Yes, I'll join in your crusade!

I had just finished up a three-week stint at **ROCKY** at the Winter Garden when the Imperial came calling once again. They needed a fill-in ticket taker for two months, and of course I accepted the offer. (Funny, the first preview was a Monday, after I'd finished a Sunday matinee at **ROCKY**. A couple of patrons came in, handed me their tickets and said, "Weren't you at **ROCKY** yesterday? You get around," they said. Ha, they had no idea.) Anyway, The Belasco would soon be re-opening and I'd go back home for that theatre's next show, but for now I was back at the Imperial. I guess I'm lucky in seemingly to always find work, and it's appreciated that the company had such trust in me. And unlike ushering at the Imperial, ticket taking is less stressful.

I remember opening night of **LES MISERABLES** 3.0 distinctly. It was a Sunday night curtain time, 6:00 pm. I woke up that morning feeling sick. Like, really sick. How the heck was I going to work this opening? But how the heck was I going to call out on such an important night? Well, you drink plenty of fluids, take lots of medication, chicken soup and bullion, etc, and you sleep for as long as you can. I guess I was feeling more myself that night, because not only did I arrive for work and get through it, I had a great time at the party at the Metropolitan Club off Fifth Avenue and 60th Street. I also got to hang with Sir Cameron, the show's legendary producer, in the lobby during the show! He's always very nice to the house staff and he was wearing a really nice blue suit. I told him so. He said thanks with that charming British smile.

That opening had Broadway and West End favorite Ramin Karimloo starring as Valjean. I would later return to the Imperial a year and a half later, after the Belasco closed. By then, Ramin had departed, replaced by another star of the West End, Alfie Boe. For another three months, I got to hear that soaring, sonorous voice (when he was in; not going beyond that). I also saw, in the original run, Lea Salonga play Eponine. In the second revival, we had Broadway talents like Keala Settle, Will Swenson, Nikki M. James, Andy Mientus, and Caissie Levy. They sold that show, with both tickets and emotion.

For my **LES MIZ** fix, I still have the London Cast and French concept album, both on vinyl, the 3-disc International Symphonic Recording on CD, the Broadway cast digitally, plus the 25th Anniversary DVD from Royal Albert Hall. Watch the four Valjean's at the end!

As I write this, memories flood back, just a little fall of rain accompanies them. They might be tears.

DIARY TWENTY-NINE

# I Put on Some Make-Up

Let's have some fun with this one. We'll talk in code. NPH, AR, MCH, JCM, DC, TD. Wait, why am I speaking in acronyms? Well, if you're a fan of **HEDWIG AND THE ANGRY INCH**, you know exactly what all those initials stand for, and it served as a form of shorthand during the 18-month run of the one of best times I've ever had working on Broadway.

So, let's put on some make-up, turn up the 8-track, and pull a wig down from the shelf. It's time to recount the origins of love for this iconic, offbeat, indulgent, funny, powerful, life-affirming show. (Are those enough adjectives? Probably not.) It's gonna take three entries to give this experience at the Belasco justice, and even then, it's no doubt not enough. For now, just enjoy the car wash.

I first came to know of this "little" show **HEDWIG AND THE ANGRY INCH** when it was playing off-Broadway in the '90s. A co-worker friend at my publishing job had connections at the box office at the Jane Street Theatre, and soon enough a group of us were headed downtown (well, we already worked in Soho, so it wasn't that far to travel) to witness this ground-breaking show. It had been playing a couple of years and many people had come and gone. John Cameron Mitchell, the show's co-creator, played the lead at the start. Even "The Breakfast Club" star Ally Sheedy played it for a run. Michael Cerveris, too. I checked my *Playbill* —I saw Matt McGrath as Hedwig.

I loved the rock score, the melodies, driving and strong and memorable and tuneful. (Yup, more adjectives.) And then came the feature film, which I saw with friends Phil and Liz in the cinema. I loved it even more. Little did I know this little show would eventually have a huge impact on my life. It was announced that **HEDWIG AND THE ANGRY INCH** would play on Broadway in the Spring of 2014, with Neil Patrick Harris in the lead role after the conclusion of his hit show, "How I Met Your Mother."

Doogie! Barney Stinson! The Tony Awards Award host! Oh, I had a feeling this was gonna be the biggest hit I'd ever worked at the Belasco, and I was right. After many years of short runs of "acclaimed productions," numerous flops and canceled bookings, the curtain was ready to rise again on a hit for the ages. You could feel the energy pulsing on West 44$^{th}$ Street even before the first preview, as evidenced by the line of people waiting for tickets, either at the box office or waiting (impatiently) for standing room "seats". The entire Belasco front of house staff was so excited, ushers, bartenders, our house manager, porters, cleaners, box office, and yup me, the lone ticket taker. It was palpable.

We began with an invited dress rehearsal. Eager theatergoers lining up outside the Belasco for our 7:00 pm pre-preview. Certain sections of the orchestra were off limits to the public, as we had reserved seating for producers and creative staff. But that didn't stop the crowd from filing in and filling in the seats and coming to life the moment NPH (that's Neil) came down from the rafters and onto the blown-out car's roof, a major set-piece. Seems **THE HURT LOCKER: THE MUSICAL** had closed on opening night and left behind some remnants. There were even discarded *Playbill*s from that show.

(This was fictional. It was a gag, part of the show.)

Then we were off, singing, dancing, laughing, cavorting, snarking (is that word?) and chances are the patrons were doing it. The cast, too. Sure, NHP was the headliner and drove ticket sales, but the second character of Yitzhak was played by Lena Hall in a career-defining role. Then there was the band, in the show called The Angry Inch, in real-life named Tits of Clay. Matt, Tim, Peter, and Justin. Talented guys and super nice. More on them later and the special thing they did for me.

**HEDWIG** was a smash hit. The reviews were through the roof that NPH came down from. Sold-out every performance, with the line for standing-room forming in the early morning, even though those tickets didn't go on sale on a first come-first serve basis until an hour before curtain. There were times I had to help manage the line with the assistance of the box office folks. I had to be tough, take a count of how many were in line, all while knowing how many SR tickets we had to sell. Sometimes the backstage folks reserved them. (Um, sometimes I did, too.) Sorry, I had a job to do and the demand was high. But I did make some great friends along the way, regulars who were huge fans of the show.

But the run was mostly fun, and I remember some especially memorable nights. A couple arrived late, about 10 minutes into the show, and their seats where in the second row, dead center. The usher took them down at the producer-approved time, but NPH paused the show while he waited for them to settle. He then addressed them, asking where they were from. "Florida," was the response. His? In character, he said, "Well, I came from (expletive) Germany, and I made it on time." (He said the entire f-word.) The crowd roared.

Another time—it was summer —there were two empty seats down front, so NPH called two guys down from the SR locations. They went racing down the aisle so fast, they had forgotten to put back on their flip-flops they had taken off at the start of the show. Our house manager did not like this, as it violates NYC hygiene in a public place. See the things we have to deal with? I remember looking at those two sets of flops while on stage, watching a hit.

This is getting long, so let me wrap up Part 1 with a great story. It was the summer of 2014 and one of the social issues that was all the rage was the ALS ice-bucket challenge. As my father had passed away from this horrible, debilitating disease in 2010, I wanted to do my part to contribute to the cause. With the permission of the house manager, I was going to get a bucket of ice water dumped on me in the Belasco alley at the end of a Friday night show. I was even wearing a Hedwig T-shirt I'd bought for social media purposes. Spread the word, find a cure.

Here's where it got interesting. The guys from Tits of Clay heard about my after-show plan and offered to dump the bucket over me. So, there I am, standing in front of the fire escape in the alley of the Belasco, with the band on the stairs standing behind me. I had the moment filmed by Eduardo. JCM, among others, were among the audience. As were some friends of Kevin Spacey (he'd gone backstage after watching the show). One of his friends saw me with the bucket and said, "Hey, he's doing the bucket challenge."

What an honor for my dad, whose passing coincides with the exact same date the Belasco reopened after a year-and-a-half renovation. October 8, 2010, saw the first show to play the newly renovated Belasco, **WOMEN ON THE VERGE OF A NERVOUS BREAKDOWN**. I of course wasn't there until the next week. But a couple years later, I got to merge both stories into a forever life-memory.

There will be more about NPH and subsequent Hedwig's in the following diary entries. It was an eventful run…but we're not done yet.

DIARY THIRTY

## Turn Up the 8-Track

Part 2 of the **HEDWIG** trilogy begins here. We're still at the Belasco Theatre, still enjoying the fun of **HEDWIG AND THE ANGRY INCH**, continuing our story of this revelatory musical and its Broadway success. It ended up being the theatre's second-longest run in its 100+-year history. That was reason enough to celebrate, so hey, the producers embraced that, never shying away from raising a glass to their success. So, hey, wanna go to a party (or several?)

**HEDWIG** with NPH was originally scheduled as a limited run. But great reviews and a bunch of Tony nominations got the producers thinking beyond the announced closing to find their next star. It was almost a case of **HOW I MET YOUR NEXT HEDWIG. HEDWIG** would go on to receive eight Tony nominations, including Best Musical Revival, Best Actor for NPH and Best Featured Actress for Lena. While being placed in the revival category caused some debate (since it had never-before played Broadway), it was a known theatrical entity. But it fell within the established rules of the Tony committee for revival.

To celebrate the myriad of nominations, the producers had a champagne-filled party in the basement of the Belasco and of course lots of VIPs were joining in on the fun. The front of house was not invited, except I was invited by one of the producers. See, I had a visible position manning the lobby of the Belasco and I got to meet various members of the creative staff that way and they recognized, and respected, the job I did.

One of my duties during the show was to prevent anyone from entering the theatre through our access door from the lobby that led into the seating area toward the end of the show. That's where Yitzhak went through a costume change (and where I made good friends with Perfidia, her dresser!) behind a curtain on the orchestra level. Our security person (usually Annie, sometimes Jerry) was downstairs to prevent patrons from going up the stairs to the seats. I had to stop people trying to enter through the lobby. Which included on the night of the Tony party the lead producer of the show and the chairman of the Shubert Organization.

Um, gulp. How can I stop them from entering? But they understood when I explained what was going on right inside that door. Phew, I'd done my job responsibly and wasn't in trouble for overstepping my bounds. The producer turned around and went through the stage door instead (not my purview), while the boss stayed with me, and we got to talking. I'd told him I'd started in the balcony at this theatre, made my way down to the mezz, then orchestra, then finally to the ticket taker position. A nice chance to let the powers that be know I'd been around a while!

I told him, "I worked my way down and out."

With a smirk, he said he wasn't sure that was the best way to phrase it. But hey, that's the perception from front of house.

So, let's get back to the celebration, the pop of the champagne bottle a signal that we were an unqualified hit. But more fun was had at the Tony Awards party, where both **HEDWIG** and **OF MICE AND MEN** (same producers) had reason to celebrate. **HEDWIG** won three Tonys, including NPH and Lena. It was held on the rooftop bar of a club in the West 30s, and yes, the entire gang was invited, cast, crew, FOH. We were fast becoming a family. Because as it turned out, we were gonna be sticking around.

NPH extended his run until mid-August. People were buying counterfeit tickets on Manhattan street-corners at 14th and 8th Avenue, only to be turned away by my scanners because they were, well, they were counterfeit. I felt bad for the fans; one turned-away woman was literally crying in the lobby as I continued to scan legitimate tickets for that matinee. Other people were camping out overnight in front of the Belasco in tents, reclining beach chairs, pillows. Some were ordering pizza, to be delivered to them on the sidewalk. I'd never seen such a devoted group of fans.

NPH departed the show, but **HEDWIG'S** run was thankfully far from over. Broadway veteran Andrew Rannells put on the make-up next for an eight-week run and he was so much fun. He could sing, act, dance, do improv, he was everything you wanted in a show like this. AR turned out to be my personal favorite of the Hedwigs. (But I'm sure many fans would disagree.) Everyone has their favorite. It's part of the joy of **HEDWIG**.

Speculation ran rampant in the aisles and backstage about who would be coming in next after AR finished out his contract. Turned out to be Michael C. Hall (MCH) of "Six Feet Under" fame. My manager and I met him at a late-night concert being performed by Tits of Clay, he against the wall, alone, quiet. Yeah, I found him shy, but very nice and unassuming when we spoke with him. When he started in the show, he was like the Swiss watch of **HEDWIG**, always coming down at the same time every night. I remember one night my now ex-Eduardo and three friends were in the box on house right where Hedwig would always toy with the audience members seated there. This night they were wearing pink and purples wigs and make-up. MCH didn't know what to make of them, what to do with them. Or respond to them. The moment fell flat.

But he was really good in the role, nonetheless. MCH, not Eduardo. (Ha!)

Then came the news: our next Hedwig would be none other than the creator, original star, the man, the myth, the star of the off-Broadway original run and the movie. Yes, John Cameron Mitchell himself (JCM). Now, as the guy who worked the lobby, I'd encountered JCM and his co-creator and composer Stephen Trask many times, and both couldn't have been sweeter to me. It was fun talking with them. Kind of awe-inspiring when they would ask me about the audience's reaction on a given night.

But when JCM started his run, that all changed. He was focused, all business, he had a job to do, and that's fine. I'd do the same. One thing I looked forward to with each new arriving Hedwig was an impromptu visit from our original lead, NHP, always showing up with a minute to spare of curtain time. With AR, he gave me a head nod. With MCH, he gave me a fist-pump. With JCM, we'd reached hugging status. I guess as Hedwigs came and went, I was the constant. And I was, and I loved it.

Then came the fateful night of the knee injury! At a 7:00 pm Saturday night show, JCM injured his knee. He persevered through the pain and finished the show, but the 10:00 pm show had to be canceled. He just couldn't go on and there was no understudy. The house manager and I worked the line of ticket holders, informing the (disappointed, sometimes belligerent) crowd what had happened and why the show wasn't happening that night. When all was said and done, the glass(es?) of wine helped us both decompress from the off-stage drama. Thanks, Saju Bistro.

MCH would return for a week to allow JCM to heal. That's a trouper and team player! It was an altered show when JCM returned, his torn meniscus limiting his mobility. He spent a lot of time on a wooden stool. But he did the show, nightly, and the crowd still loved seeing the original. **HEDWIG** remained a hot ticket, but it also had us all wondering, once again, who the next Hedwig would be, or if the show could be closing.

With glee, we'd found our next Hedwig. Stay tuned. (Boop.) Turn the page.

## DIARY THIRTY-ONE

# Pull the Wig Down From the Shelf

For those of you in the know, you do realize I dropped an obvious hint at the end of the last diary about the next Hedwig to play the Belasco. One of the breakout stars of the hit Fox TV show "Glee" was bringing his talents—and his fervent fans —to the Belasco. I of course mean Darren Criss.

Again, there came lots of speculation about whether Darren was the right choice, was he too young to understand the paths and pathos this character had experienced? I admit I was among those early skeptics initially. Sure, DC went through some growing pains in the role in the first couple of weeks, but I have to say, I've rarely seen an actor realize the challenge in front of him and embrace it until he got it—and beyond.

DC was terrific, all while bringing in a different demographic to the show. NPH was a hot ticket, Hollywood royalty, ticket prices higher than...well, **HAMILTON** hadn't yet arrived, but you get the idea. Lots of Manhattan people of privilege were buying up tickets from brokers who knew how to bilk their audience. AR, he brought in the insider-Broadway crowd, he fresh off **THE BOOK OF MORMON** insanity. MCH drew in the suburban audiences, mainly the ladies; I mean, he was Dexter! JCM's audience were the Hedwigians of yesteryear, eager to see the star and creator recreate his iconic role. And now, there was this "kid."

Here's where I'll take a time-out from talking about our Hedwigs and discuss instead our audience. While performing my job, here's how it goes down: you work a show, you greet the patrons, scan their tickets, get them seated, make sure they have a memorable time, hope to see you at another show. Uh, not so with **HEDWIG**. I'd see the crowd not just for another show, I'd see them for the NEXT performance! Meaning they'd be back the next night, or the night after, or for two shows over the weekend. I didn't get the fixation on the show at first.

It's a delicate balance between doing your job and enforcing the rules you've been instructed upon by your bosses and building a relationship with a devoted audience who showed up like locusts on the last day of the world. Like I said, since I worked the lobby during the complete run of the show, I had to tread these waters lightly. We had one security person working alongside me, the fabulous Annie, without whom I'd never have survived this show. We were a team, trying to find a way to please the crowd and maintain the operation of the theatre.

She would set up the barricades at the stage door for fans who wanted autographs after the show. But there were nights when people not seeing the show came into the lobby requesting *Playbills*. I had been given strict instructions from the producers not to hand out programs to those not attending the show. Because those people would just linger in front of the theatre, taking up space amidst the barricades, stealing spots from paying customers. Usually security handled this, but during the costume change at the end of the show Annie would be downstairs, so it was left to me to direct the crowd to where they could stand. Some message boards weren't kind to me.

Okay, let's bring this DC back into the story. This is fun. My college-age cousin Samantha, who invented the phrase "Cousin Uncle Joe" wanted to come to the show with her friend, a huge DC fan. I checked with the box office staff and they secured me some rush seats down front. Also present in the box office when placing the order was DC's assistant, the lovely Eleni. She said, 'Do they want to meet Darren after the show?"

It was a matinee performance they were attending, and DC had another show that Saturday night. He usually didn't see people between shows; you gotta get your rest! But Eleni made it happen. Samantha and her friend got to meet him and take pictures with him, and I even got in on the action. A class act, DC, right there. (Fun fact, the first time I worked the Belasco post-Hedwig was for a lame-duck show called **GETTING THE BAND BACK TOGETHER**, and who did I seat? DC and Eleni. Hugs ensued.)

But DC would leave us, the new star revealed in the form of Broadway alum and TV star Taye Diggs. He was announced for a 13-week run, which would take us into October of 2015. For various reasons, though, I felt **HEDWIG** was losing some steam, I could sense a sea-change in the audience (and a drop in the attendance), and suddenly there it was: a closing date was posted for September 13$^{th}$, which coincided with my…birthday.

What a day that would turn out to be!

Okay, imagine pandemonium of West 44$^{th}$ Street, the kind of buzz you rarely witnessed at our east of Broadway locale. But it was beyond exciting on that final day. As I rounded the street corner off Sixth Avenue, I ran into four of our loyal Hedwigians, each of them dressed in football jerseys…no, not Jets nor Giants fans here. The backs of those jerseys were splayed with people's last names who were associated with the show, including…Pittman. Um, I was honored and humbled.

Somehow the Hedwig gang had learned that, amidst the closing of the show, it was my birthday. Once I'd donned my TT suit to set-up the outside of the theatre for this final performance, already feeling mournful, I found myself being serenaded by everyone already gathered in front of the theatre singing "Happy Birthday" to me. I was altogether thrilled and embarrassed and touched. It was a bit like when a journalist becomes part of the story they are covering. That day should have been about what **HEDWIG** accomplished, but I was very appreciative of the fans.

Let's get to that night, Tits of Clay was performing at a venue in Brooklyn, and I wasn't anticipating to go to the show. I hadn't booked tickets, after all, but once the "show" found out it was my birthday, well, let's just say I ended up in the VIP section upstairs during the concert, and later, was dragged onto a bus for the "after party." I thought it was a private party for the band, but it turned out to be the closing night party for **HEDWIG** in the West Village. A rooftop bar again, lots of hugs and smiles and remembrances were exchanged. As I departed, I heard the notes of the final song, "Midnight Radio" thrumming through my mind. Of course, the time had grown long past that hour. That's how we do it in Manhattan.

There are other stories to tell about this show, but they relate more to the Belasco Theatre than to our **HEDWIG** friends and memories. I'll tell those in a future diary. For now, I think I'm done with recollections of this fabulous show, surely one of the most fantabolous experiences of any show I've worked. Looking back on those nights, it sure has been a long day's journey into night. Hey, wait, that's another show I worked. Wonder what happened there?

DIARY THIRTY-TWO

## Is it Mourning Yet?

Talk about a title of a play that lives up to its name! Clocking in at four hours and fifteen minutes, two intermissions, drama and strife and family mendacity, you know it's gotta be worthy of its classic status. Damn sure, that's just what it was.

And as it turned out, this production became my favorite straight play I'd ever work. My nickname for it was long night's journey into morning. But of course, it's famously called **LONG DAY'S JOURNEY INTO NIGHT**, Eugene O'Neill's Tony-winning opus, for which he was awarded, posthumously, the Pulitzer Prize. Yeah, it's that good. Rumor has it he never wanted it produced or performed, but audiences are the richer for those who defied O'Neill's wishes.

The original production in 1956 starred Fredric March, Florence Eldridge, Jason Robards Jr, and Bradford Dillman in the four major roles. It played the original Helen Hayes Theatre on 46th Street. Since then, it has enjoyed—and the audience has endured—this epic play of a tortured family all over the world, revivals playing on Broadway at the Broadhurst, the Neil Simon, and the production I'm writing about here, at the Plymouth.

But before we return to 2003, let's go back a few years earlier and my first introduction to this tour-de-force. London, 2000, the Lyric Theatre on Shaftesbury Avenue. I was staying there for a month-long writing excursion, but I also took the time out from chapters to see theatre (a lot of theatre, I think 15 shows). I looked up at that marquee, saw Charles Dance, Jessica Lange, Paul Rudd, Paul Nicholls in name and face. I knew the first three actors, the fourth a young Brit with a big young fan base (read: he was cute).

I bought a ticket, unaware of what I was in for. I had no idea of the length of the play, and after the second intermission I did think to myself how appropriate this title was. I felt like I'd been in the Lyric for days! But it was mesmerizing, with such powerful performances, each of the actors owning their roles like they were the Tyrone family. 11:30 that night, after a 7:30 start, I was drained.

Okay, cut to 2003, and here came **LONG DAY'S** journeying back into my life. A revival directed by acclaimed director Robert Falls was to take up residence at the Plymouth on 45th Street from April until August. A near-six month run of what would be the longest play I've still ever worked on Broadway. I'd lament not having a

90-minute show and getting home earlier but given our cast...sometimes you make an exception. (There was also overtime pay involved.)

Brian Dennehy, Vanessa Redgrave, Philip Seymour Hoffman, and Robert Sean Leonard. Fiana Tobin played the smaller role of the maid with fiery drive. This was not just any revival, and this wasn't just any hit. This was an EVENT. Just seven shows a week (no Wednesday matinee), curtain time in the evening was at 7:00 pm, Saturday matinee at 1:00 pm, Sunday matinee at 2:00 pm. Of all the theatres on 45$^{th}$ Street (and beyond), we were the first to open our doors and the last to close them.

Primarily I was ushering the show, but our head usher had to take time off for personal reasons, and so our directress Helen became chief, and I became director on the mezzanine level. What does that mean? That during my late shifts, I didn't always have to be on the floor watching the show and supervising the audience. Some of my director duties happened to take place in the lobby, especially between the 7:00 and 8:00 hours, when the box office was still doing future sales—ail while the show playing inside. We had to ask the customers to wait outside the lobby on the sidewalk until it was their turn to talk to the box office person, quietly, at the window. There wasn't much space between our lobby and the first set of seats inside the theatre. What the ticket taker and I had to do was noise control.

I remember one night, we had a long line (well, we usually did) and this one gentleman came to me and demanded he be accelerated to the front of the line. He claimed he was a Broadway producer and should not have to be subjected to this line. When I denied his request, he insisted with a first-world mentality that I seek out the house manager to rectify the situation. I went upstairs to his office and told our manager of the situation. I was informed I could handle it; no way was this abusive customer getting his way. When I informed him he'd have to wait, the man stormed away in anger, but not before asking for my name and threatening to call the Shuberts and complain about me.

Maybe it was safer inside the theatre watching the show.

Anyway, there were many good times working there. I always liked seeing Philip Seymour Hoffman smoking cigarettes outside the stage door—during the show! He had a long break before he was needed to be back on stage. I remember during previews our lead producer compiling a list of the names of all front-of-house employees. Next thing we know we've all got **LONG DAY'S JOURNEY INTO NIGHT** show jackets, black denim, the show's logo on the back, but with our individual names stitched on the front—just like everyone else associated with show. A classy move. It meant we were as much a part of this as everyone else. That doesn't always occur.

Last fun story, Act III had begun, the house lights had

gone down, and this woman returns from the restroom, hesitating at the top of the aisle. She was nervous to go back down to her seat in the dark and disturb people. But this was the only chance I had to get her back, as the final act, as I informed her, was over an hour in length. As I escorted her down the center aisle with my flashlight, I learned she was in the middle of the row, next to her date Lenny Kravitz. She was so fearful Page Six of the *New York Post* would find out about her transgression. I told her to blame it on the usher. She touched my arm and said, "Thanks."

The woman was Nicole Kidman. She was very sweet.

Okay, another story. One Saturday matinee we came to the theatre to discover that Ms. Redgrave was not going to be performing for the rest of the weekend. Sadly, her mother, Rachel Kempson, had passed away. This was our first understudy to go on, and it turned out, I was familiar with the actress going on that day, Pamela Payton-Wright. She played the recurring role of Addie Cramer on "One Life to Live"! (One of my favorite shows ever; sister to the awesome Dorian Lord.)

But perhaps the most memorable experience of working this show was the night we ended up not even having a show. The fateful date? August 14th, 2003, New York City (and much of the Northeast) was hit with a massive blackout. It was around 4:00 pm when the lights went out. Not sure what to do, the battery on my cell phone dying, I just decided to head to work. Surely this was temporary. I started to walk through the strangely silent streets of Manhattan, not quite dark yet because it was daytime. I looked at everyone else on the streets and it was clear this blackout was a big deal. No subways were running, no lights, no…nothing but nothing. I figured by the time I finished my hour-long journey into night the power would be back by curtain time.

I walked 45 blocks to the Plymouth, only to be told by the house manager to turn around. No power, no show. So, I walked another 45 blocks back uptown. August heat. Manhattan cement. No air conditioning. Fun times! That night, Eugene O'Neill truly gave his title, not quiet light, but life, in the fact that all of New York was experiencing a long day's journey into night…and beyond.

Thanks for reading this entry. If I'm writing about O'Neill, it had to go on for a while. But hey, he started it.

DIARY THIRTY-THREE

## To Kong, With Love

I wasn't intending to write this entry at this point in my story, but on second thought it does seems appropriate as I look back on the date. As of this writing, this coincides with the second anniversary of the closing of **KING KONG** at the Broadway Theatre (August 18th, 2019, officially) I've got a lot of complex emotions and memories over this one.

After **HEDWIG**, and a three-month stint as one of the two ticket takers at the Imperial Theatre, I was "offered," according to the email from the Shubert office, the Broadway Theatre as my new home. The Shubert's largest house at 1,761 seats, it was thought by many, including me, to be a major promotion. That theatre got big shows, so big in fact, that it could house a helicopter and, as it turned out, a monster-sized ape! But I'm getting ahead of myself.

I was presented with the second ticket taker spot at this theatre, filling in for someone who could no longer perform the job due to a terminal medical issue. I knew him, I liked him, he was a great guy and I enjoyed when he would stop by the theatre just to say hello to his friends. Sadly, he passed away during the pandemic. But it was an honor to fill his shoes for what turned into a five-year job. Louis, grab those stars.

But back to **KING KONG**. When the show was announced, Broadway know-it-alls started wagging their gossipy tongues. Horrible idea! Major flop! Have Producers Gone Bananas? I'll tell you the truth: I liked **KONG**; in fact, I liked it a lot. Was it a perfect musical? No. Was the score memorable? Hmm, only slightly. Was King Kong himself awesome? Beyond a doubt. An absolute marvel of stagecraft and technology, and thanks to his handlers, on stage and behind the scenes, he had such personality!

Also, did they have the best merchandise items for sale? I love my **KING KONG** plush toy. (So does Shadow, but I don't let him play with it, because he'd tear it to shreds.) Katie, our merchandise manager for the run of the show, I write that comment in your memory. I keep the magnet I bought from the show on our fridge!

Previews of **KING KONG** began on October 8, 2018, with a splashy opening at Rockefeller Center a month later, on November 8. We were all part of the celebration, cast, crew, FOH, one big happy, crazy Kong-obsessed family. The only one who failed to make an appearance at the party was the star himself, Kong; perhaps he was just having some banana daiquiris backstage in a quiet moment after such build-up. Yeah, he was an animatronic puppet, but he was so real, and you felt for how he was treated—abused —by the characters for his exhibitionism. He was our tortured hero.

Even if he did breakdown sometimes and cause delays during the show. That's show biz.

Major props to the crew and the many Kong puppeteers for the awesome work they did in bringing him to life—and sometimes back to life. But, yeah, it wasn't always smooth sailing. He broke down a couple times during previews and we'd have to bring the house lights up and allow patrons to get up and use the restrooms. "When will it resume," I would be asked. I wasn't going to monkey around, so I said, honestly, that I didn't know. One night a piece of scenery fell on the stage from above and the cast went dashing off the stage, not to return that night. We had to cancel the rest of the performance. (Everyone was thankfully fine; it was not a **SHOGUN: THE MUSICAL** moment, where actor Philip Casnoff was injured.) I'll resist saying the audience went ape when we had to escort them out of the theatre.

Another night, there was a rolling blackout all along Broadway, the street. It was a Saturday night and we had just opened the house to our audience and had begun the process of scanning tickets when the lights went down. Full on dark. The house manager said to close the doors after we'd cleared the house, waiting for word from stage management on whether we'd have a show that night. The staff was instructed to head across the street at a "holding area," a Bank of America vestibule. Word eventually filtered over that the performance was again cancelled. Interesting fact: the only shows that went up that night were located east of Broadway, and funnily enough, they all began with the letter B: **BEETLEJUICE, BE MORE CHILL, BLACKBIRD,** and **BEAUTIFUL** The power outage was a West Side issue.

**KING KONG** the show had its detractors, but what I found working the front door was that it had its eager fans. Families were coming to see the show, often many of these young kids making their own Broadway debut. Boys in particular, because a lot of family shows are "girl-centric." The Broadway League was, at the time, running a great promotion to welcome new theatregoers. Was this your first time on Broadway? If so, you could get a free double sticker, one you could slap on your shirt, another on your *Playbill* for posterity.

I wore the sticker myself on my suit lapel and would point to it when I saw little kids, and I'd direct them to the merchandise booth (who handed them out) if it was their first time seeing a Broadway show. The appreciation I'd get from the parents and kids made my day: you want them to remember their first time seeing live theatre. It brings them back to experience life upon our stages as they grow older. That's how you build an audience.

More fun memories of life at **KONG**. Outside of my theatre life, I'm a news junkie, (Hey, I was a journalism major in college and am a writer) and in particular I'm an ABC News guy. Always have been, going all the way back to college when I watched "Good Morning, America," religiously —and still do. Our female lead in **KONG**, Christiani Pitts, is the daughter of "Nightline" co-anchor Byron Pitts, and I guess he encouraged several of his colleagues to come see the show. I got to say hi to TJ Holmes, Juju Chang, and Whit Johnson, among others. Worlds colliding! My mornings coming to my nights.

And then there was our human leading man, Eric William Morris, who I first met while we were both working at Circle in the Square. I was ushering, he was doing the headsets, but what we had in common was the pursuit of other, well, pursuits. I stayed with the writing, while he sought the stage. He'd eventually book a short-lived drama called **CORAM BOY** at the Imperial, and later, **MAMMA MIA** at the Winter Garden. To watch him command the Broadway Theatre stage made for a great story of fulfilling a dream.

**KING KONG** also had a big impact on my personal life. I'd moved from NY to NJ, Steve and I adopted the most adorable dog (yes, MOST adorable), Shadow. Shadow and Kong possessed a symbiotic relationship in my mind; both had entered my life at the right time. I also have to give a shout out to the front of house staff of the Broadway, who were thoughtful enough to throw me a wedding shower the week before my nuptials. That was unexpected, and exciting, but in the end, a bittersweet moment. I'd leave that theatre under less-than-ideal circumstances—more on that in a later entry.

But even as the wedding neared, this was also a sad time. The closing notice had gone up on **KING KONG**, set for two weeks after my wedding. I'd miss a few shows for our big event, but I'd be back for the final performances. I wasn't missing that! On the day of the final performance, I finally got to meet my buddy Kong up close, right up there on stage before the show. One of our stagehands was gracious enough to take a few photos. I'll treasure them forever.

There are so many other stories to tell. My best friend Mike and his husband Joey, who flew in from Los Angeles for the wedding, attended the show the Friday night before the Sunday celebration. The company manager of **KONG** was gracious enough to provide me (well, them) with a complimentary set of tickets in honor of the big day. We met the cast on the stage after the show and Christiani, when finding out I was getting married in two days, gave me a huge hug and wished me a happy day. When I returned a few days later to the show, Christiani was like, "Well, how'd it go?" I just flashed my ring. Another hug. She's so sweet.

There was also the entire Stagecoach Tavern gang, a nearby pub, an establishment that welcomed me like family as I sat there between shows to write my books. I reciprocated and treated them like family at the Broadway for **KONG**. Teena, Izzy, Cevin, Loretta,

Michelle, I'd get them rush seats and then, if available, upgrade them. I remember some patrons watching us as I moved them down to house seats. It was almost like they were saying, "Who are they, who is he?" They were my VIPs, that's who. So was John, a conductor who would often check my ticket on NJ Transit, usually on the weekends—he and his wife came to see the show and I moved them too.

Ok, one last story, but a good one. My friends Phil and Liz have two beautiful and talented daughters, Jessica and Lauren, who love Broadway—and their "Uncle Joe." Back at you. One night I scored them rush tickets for **KONG**, then was able to move them down to better seats, again, house seats. At the end of the show, I had asked stage management if it was okay to take them on the stage. Approval granted, they got to meet Eric and Christiani. Alas, Kong had been relegated to his holding place high above the stage, where once **MISS SAIGON**'s helicopter had lived for 10 years.

While King Kong entered my life first, my beloved Shadow is now my Kong, another furry black animal filled with such sweetness and personality and presence. But in truth, their symbiotic relationship is never-ending, each of them filling me with memories of insightful eyes and a gentle touch of a paw. Thank goodness Shadow doesn't require me to climb the Empire State Building to battle those attacking planes. I just must deal with the vagaries of Jersey Transit.

And with that, I let out one last roar. For a show so maligned in the press, it sure had its fans—count me in —and so many of my friends were eager to come through my doors at the the Broadway Theatre. To Kong, with love, while you'll always remain king of the jungle, know that for nearly a year you were the King of Broadway, too. You were my favorite show during those days, nights, when I worked at the Broadway.

DIARY THIRTY-FOUR

# The Berlin Secret

Sounds like a spy novel, that chapter title, doesn't it? But in fact, it's just the inevitable happening, finding my way back to 45$^{th}$ Street again, a place we've (I've) been to many times over all these years. And why not, there are so many theatres on this stretch of midtown between Broadway and 8$^{th}$ Avenue: Booth, Schoenfeld, Jacobs, Golden, the Imperial and...this chapter's theatre feature: The Music Box.

This theatre has an interesting history that goes way back to 1920, and one I was not a part of for much of my ushering/ticket taking career. That would eventually change, and I was so glad to finally get to call this theatre a once-a-week home, kind of like a weekly slice of comfort food. Okay, let me explain the complicated history.

See, back when I started ushering, the Music Box had been co-owned, half by The Shubert Organization and half by the Estate of songwriter and icon Irving Berlin. They had their own rules, their own staff, even their own usher outfits that defied what the rest of us Shubert folks wore. While the women of Shubert wore all black, the male ushers were required to wear white dress shirts along with black ties (at first), and later the now-iconic that encompasses all the 17 theatre marquees—all set against an azure background. And that tie included the Music Box marquee, even though they didn't—and still don't—wear them. The Music Box, also, oddly, tended to hire only male ushers and they too were all dressed in black. No white shirts there. (Lucky them!)

Having worked across the street from this theatre at the then-named Plymouth Theatre, I knew some of the staff and I would watch as the marquee changed with each new show that came in. I'd even see a few. Rodgers and Hammerstein's **STATE FAIR**, **BLOOD BROTHERS** (I love that show!), the short-lived **SWINGING ON A STAR**, a big hit in London-big flop in NYC play called **FESTEN** (with Ali MacGraw, with whom I'd worked with in my publishing life), and a misguided **MACBETH** with Kelsey Grammer (also, with whom I'd worked with in my publishing life). **THE DINNER PARTY** played there with John Ritter and Henry Winkler. The 70s were alive with pleasure.

But I'd yet to walk its aisles as an usher, a stack of *Playbill*s in my hand.

One of my long-time union pals, I'll call him...uh, John, he was working there on Aisle 1 and he helped get me set up at the Music Box with the longtime head usher...uh, I'll call him Dennis. I was working **HEDWIG** at the time and I to gain another shift I benefited by the fact we never had Wednesday matinee performances at the Belasco. So, I secured a regular gig: an every Wednesday matinee shift at the Music Box.

But what was the show? That was the true selling point of my weekly assignment. The new revival of **PIPPIN**. I have a history with this music, having performed various songs from it in high school chorale. Once this show was announced for a Broadway return, I knew I had to see it, and see it I did, wasting no time at all by attending the second preview on a Sunday night, walking over after my matinee of **THE NANCE** at the Lyceum. The actress Andrea Martin was part of our audience that afternoon at the Lyceum, and as I scanned her ticket, I informed her I was attending her show that night. She replied by saying, "Why, don't we both have busy days today."

But back to my regular Wednesday matinee assignment. I loved this production of **PIPPIN**: Patina Miller as the Leading Player, and by the time I started working it, Kyle Dean Massey was playing the title role; Rachel Bay Jones remained in the show, along with Terrence Mann and Charlotte d'Amboise (husband and wife). What a treat to hear this fabulous score every week, and to watch Ms. Martin dangle upside-down on the trapeze as she sang "No Time at All"—complete with an audience sing-along! The words of the chorus were projected from the stage for all the audience to see—and participate.

I worked this show for a year, and I watched as several cast changes were made. One of my favorite additions was Lucie Arnaz, who came in to replace Ms. Martin. Finding the strength within me, I walked down to the lip of the stage where she was rehearsing and introduced myself as one of the ushers. Then I told her I had seen her perform in the musical of **THE WITCHES OF EASTWICK** at Theatre Royal/Drury Lane in London. That impressed her! She'd wave to me each week after that.

**PIPPIN** would close, as most shows eventually do, but my Wednesday gig remained at the Music Box Theatre. I would next work the misguided revival of **THE HEIDI CHRONICLES**. I've got nothing against Elisabeth Moss, who held her own dealing with a dated script, including a great performance of her character's big speech toward the end of the show; I also enjoyed working again with Jason Biggs (**THE GRADUATE**), who's always a friendly guy. But I disliked the very busy and over-set production.

I'd also work, once, **SHUFFLE ALONG**, which I felt was disjointed and lacked a clear point of view despite having a very strong cast, and, again, once, **DEAR EVAN HANSEN**, which I liked but didn't go crazy over as so many others have. I like the score, not the book. That's often my issue with musicals.

An intriguing show that came to the Music Box was a British import called **KING CHARLES III**. A "what-if" play from London, following the events that happened after the death of Queen Elizabeth II and Prince Charles's ascension to the throne; but there were all sorts of palace intrigue about William, Kate, and Harry (pre-Meghan). Written like a Shakespeare tragedy, it was thrilling theatre and I was absorbed. Again, give me something well-written and I'm in.

I remember one Wednesday afternoon the manager Jonathan asked me to do a favor for him. There were some VIPS in the audience, influential Broadway producers. Would I mind, at intermission, taking them upstairs to the manager's office so they could relax without the crowd around them? Um, sure. See, there's a bit of lore about that office: it was Irving Berlin's, and it has some stories about the long-ago past about it. I'm going to respect the secret history and not reveal all. I'll just give a hint: Prohibition and an icebox.

That was a treasured moment, and I felt thankful to be entrusted with such a task. I felt I'd truly made my mark at the Music Box after all those years of just looking across the street at its green lettering. I loved setting up my stacks of *Playbills* on Aisle 1, donning the usher outfit, which included a purple paisley tie, grabbing my flashlight, and hearing the words, "The house is open." It's the thrill before the curtain rises. There's a song in **PIPPIN** called "Morning Glow" that closes out Act I. For me, my weekly trip to the Music Box was Afternoon Glow.

## DIARY THIRTY-FIVE

# Let There Be Peace on Earth

We all have our memories of that day of infamy, 20 years ago as of this writing. What has become defined by all as, simply, sadly, 9/11. A day that would change the world, alter us all, much like Pearl Harbor must have done to the Greatest Generation. Infamy, indeed. I—as a New Yorker—was left with an indelible series of images from not just the events of that tragic Tuesday morning but of its effect on Broadway. All of it seared in my mind, then, now, forever.

It's useful to set the scene, and to do that, we back up to that summer of 2001. The Plymouth Theatre went dark after a revival of the classic **BELLS ARE RINGING** failed to catch on with audiences (and critics). I'll write about that show in another chapter. Anyway, I found work at one of my favorite theatres, Circle in the Square, located at 50$^{th}$ Street between Broadway and 8$^{th}$. The show? The acclaimed and totally fun revival of **THE ROCKY HORROR SHOW**.

Imagine a Broadway line-up of talent like this: Tom Hewitt, Dick Cavett, Raul Esparza, Daphne Rubin-Vega,

Joan Jett, Lea Delaria, Jarrod Emick and Alice Ripley. Dammit, Janet, that's great casting, and great fun. When I began working the show, Jarrod had taken a leave and in came a bit of celebrity casting: that 90210 heartthrob Dylan, Luke Perry himself. He sure helped fill our 750-seat theatre with screaming fan-girls.

But we had plenty of other fans, mostly those of the midnight showings of the movie.

The show was selling well anyway. Repeat customers, usually in costume, lots of expected-by-the-cast audience participation, gift bags available for purchase filled with all the accoutrements you'd need to toss during appropriate times and lines, at the cast. Everyone knew the catch phrases which produced comebacks from the audience (Gleem!); the atmosphere at Circle was one big party. I was having a blast working this show. Pure indulgence, fun, laughter, a rocking score and an energetic cast and a great staff to work with. I felt part of the Circle family.

I spent all of June, July and August at this theatre, and then came September. The Plymouth was gearing up for its new show at the end of the month, but I would continue to work Circle in the Square until then. How the world often has other ideas.

My first memory from that fateful day on 9/11 comes two days earlier, on 9/9. I was just getting off the subway, headed to my apartment between our two Sunday shows. Some rowdy kids were playing in front of their apartment building on 87th Street between 3rd and 2nd Avenues and they taunted me a bit as I walked by. When I ignored them, one of the kids threw a rock at me; it missed. But I clearly recall thinking how sad the world had become.

Prescient, maybe only the universe knows. But I felt a shift occur within myself, and then, on a day that rose with a warm, radiant late-summer blue sky, I woke up to the worst news. A call from my sister informing me that someone had crashed a plane into the one of the towers of the World Trade Center. I switched on the television to "Good Morning, America," and watched as New York City burned. I cried and wondered: how, and why. The inevitable call came in from my head usher at Circle, Georgia: no show tonight.

Of course not, who could sing and dance and do the "Time Warp" while all you wanted to do was rewind to the previous day. What theater patron would venture out from the needed security of their home on such a day? But you know, eventually we had to, we needed to.

We returned to performances two days later, on 9/13, doing so at the urging of our at-the-time celebrated mayor (I won't speak his name) to get our city back up and running to a pre-9/11 life. Foregoing the subway, I wanted to see the city, and so I walked down the Fifth Avenue side of Central Park, headed to Circle that Thursday afternoon, smelling the acrid smoke as it hovered over the quiet streets and avenues. Knowing the tragedy was still unfolding at the lower tip of my beloved Manhattan, pondering the concept of taking a song from **ROCKY HORROR** and having the entire city do that "Time Warp." More than a jump to the left, how about a jump back in time?

Word came down that on Friday night a candlelight vigil was being held all over the city at 7:00 pm. Our staff assembled in front of Circle, with friends, neighbors, strangers, all of us holding candles, the flames flickering in the wind as the sun dipped beneath the smoky clouds and into the encroaching night. One of our substitute ushers, Bonnie, who also is a minister, was standing next to me, observing the silence when she suddenly burst into beautiful song. This was Broadway, after all. It was **COME FROM AWAY** before that show existed. A brief 9/11 musical.

We shared voices of unity and sorrow.

Bonnie led us into the lyrics and lilting melody of "Let There Be Peace on Earth," and soon all of those gathered around 50$^{th}$ Street and 8$^{th}$ Avenue were joined in a celebration of life, love, of perseverance, of hope for tomorrow. My heart had never swelled so much, wishing life could go back to normal, all while we celebrated those first responders who risked all to help. I include one of Circle's own staff members, our directress, a blowsy, fun-loving, giant-hearted and giving lady named Tammy. For days, she would venture down to Lower Manhattan, hold up signs that supported the

FDNY and other responders, helping to feed them too and campaign for donations. She was the epitome of a New Yorker. Tough as nails, hard talking, but comforting in a time few knew how to process.

**ROCKY HORROR**'s return date coincided with my birthday, 9/13, and after my shift (I was early that night, just did the seating), and so I was meeting with a couple of friends who had been displaced from their apartment in Battery Park City—across the street from the World Trade Center. A great pal from college and his pregnant wife, two of my best friends. Our celebration at the Stanhope Hotel on Fifth Avenue and 80th Street was subdued. How do you raise a glass in such a moment? But I appreciated the acknowledgment of another year on this earth.

**ROCKY HORROR** would put up a closing notice and play its final performance before the end of the month due to the lack of tourists coming to New York City. But then the producers announced a 10-week comeback with special guest actors, a revolving door of narrators and other characters. But by then I'd gone back to the Plymouth. I remember one Sunday morning in early October when I joined my sister and her husband for a memorial service for a friend of theirs who worked in one of the towers. I'd met him, his wife, had dinner with them and greatly enjoyed their company. I had to attend the service. But I also remember taking Metro-North back to the city in time for the 3:00 pm matinee.

The day known as 9/11 lives inside us forever, it is the city, it is us, and Broadway did its part to help us heal. What happened was a tragedy we witnessed before our eyes, but one we could fight against, and we did. Unlike today's world, where Broadway saw its lights go dark for eighteen months in the face of, this time, an invisible enemy.

I think I'd have just preferred to be hit by that rock.

Here's the final twist in this long tale. I'd first worked this production of **THE ROCKY HORROR SHOW** on December 31, 2000. We had a 10:00 pm curtain and cast, crew, staff and audience would ring in the hopeful new year together. Our backstage team lowered several large TV screens so we could watch Dick Clark's "New Year's Rockin' Eve" usher in what many thought was the dawn of a new millennium. Innocence back then, drowned out nine months later in tears and remembrance.

## DIARY THIRTY-SIX

## Circle X 3...and More

I was inspired by that last remembrance, so let's stay working at Circle in the Square and relive some happier times.

I detailed my **ROCKY HORROR** experience, and in previous diary entries covered **THE 25TH ANNUAL PUTNAM COUNTY SPELLING BEE**, as well as my first-ever show there, **ZOYA'S APARTMENT**. But there were many interesting shows which I got to work at this unique and wonderful theatre, sometimes seeing a show just once or a few times, but other times for weeks or a summer or for an extended run. Let's take another trip down the escalator and see what round peg we fit into a square.

2002. Mary Zimmerman's **METAMORPHOSES**, which transformed Circle's stage into a pool! The water temperature and chemical levels had to be maintained very carefully by the stagehands to avoid any parasites or other such pool-like issues for the cast members who were immersed in the water during the performance. Kudos to all for keeping things fresh, and the cast for a revealing, intriguing show that explored the world of mythology with such cleverness.

2003. **LIFE X 3**, Yasmina Reza's follow-up to her smash hit, **ART**. An interesting cast of four filled out the true Circle: Movie and TV stars John Turturro, Helen Hunt, Brent Spiner, and Broadway favorite Linda Emond headlined the show. It was a short-lived run, just a few months. I enjoyed watching it, but there were issues that happen when you're working a show with, um, shall we politely say: stars. We were constantly being told that a certain cast member kept telling stage management about the "distracting" ushers who were busy assisting latecomers. Not our fault people were late. We sat people according to how we were directed. How about you do your job, and we'll do ours? The cast had to eat chocolate crackers every performance. Maybe someone, and I ain't saying who, was on a sugar rush. That's as good as it gets.

2004. **FROZEN**. A fascinating play with three high-end, dedicated actors: Swoosie Kurtz, Brian F. O'Bryne, and Laila Robins. Again, not a long run, but it was embraced by the critics and Brian won the Tony for Lead Actor in a Play. I was always a fan of Laila's since I saw her perform in a short-lived play, **THE HERBAL BED**, at the O'Neill. Swoosie was awesome too, someone I knew more from television shows like "Sisters."

2008. **GLORY DAYS**. Oh my. This was the first show to take up residence at Circle in the Square after

**SPELLING BEE**'s closing, and I was scheduled to return—but I had a sense it wasn't going to last long. I'd agreed at that point to return to the Belasco for **PASSING STRANGE**, but I did get to work **GLORY DAYS** on its final preview that Monday night in April. It opened and closed the next night. Looks like I think perhaps maybe I made the right choice on that one.

2009. Hey, what about three plays that are all actually really just one play, each of them two and a half hours in length, and one that doesn't always follow a thru-storyline depending upon in which order they are performed. Anyone familiar with the genius that is British playwright Alan Ayckbourne's **THE NORMAN CONQUESTS**? With a brilliant cast of six actors, three men, three women, brought over from England, this rare production had one of the most unusual schedules I'd ever worked. On Saturday (and some Sundays), we did all three shows, with the first starting at 11:00 am, the second at 3:00, the last at 8:00. By the time we seated our same audience for that last show, most people remembered where their seats were. Ha, ushers in training. We'd say hi to them. Where did you have dinner? They'd ask the same.

Two favorite memories of **THE NORMAN CONQUESTS**: Tyne Daly came one Saturday, and I greeted her for the first show, welcomed her by name. "Ms. Daly." She was super sweet and approachable. When she returned for the matinee, she double-checked with me regarding her seat location. By the time she arrived back for the final show, she knew where to go, but she still stopped and said hello. "Long day," we agreed. But a thrilling, silly epic day of theatre. How that cast did those three shows in succession was remarkable.

Then, another Saturday three-show day at **NORMAN** arrived and so did horror writer Peter Straub, whom I'd worked with in my publishing life briefly. I knew him by sight, because I'm a big fan of his work ("Ghost Story" is a favorite of mine) and I always look at author photos. Me, not such recognition on his part. But I introduced myself and reminded him of our association and he smiled with acknowledgment. He smiled even brighter when I pulled out a paperback copy of one of his early novels, "Shadowland" from within my *Playbill* stand, which I was coincidentally reading at the time. He signed it for me right then and there! I had to ask a couple of patrons who were waiting to be seated to give me a moment.

2014. **LADY DAY**. Oh, anything Audra McDonald stars in I'm all for it. I first saw her in **CAROUSEL**, then **RAGTIME, MASTER CLASS, MARIE CHRISTINE** to name a few. And now here she was starring in the one-woman show **LADY DAY AT EMERSON'S BAR & GRILL,** her tour-de-force transformation from one glorious singer into another, Billie Holliday. The way Audra swept around Circle's unique staging was magical, with patrons seated at cabaret-like tables getting to see and hear her up close. The audience was enraptured by the intimacy of such a show.

Except for this one woman. It was a Saturday matinee; I was filling in that afternoon until my double-night shift at **HEDWIG** at 7:00 and 10:00. The show began, Audra began to sing. I think it took two songs before this woman in the last row (thankfully not the first row!), got up out of her seat. As I'm supposed to do as an usher, I asked if she was in need of assistance. Her reply couldn't have been more direct: "I came to hear Audra McDonald sing. Not this." And she left the theatre. Sometimes the audience brings the drama.

2016. **FUN HOME**. I met the author of this groundbreaking show, Alison Bechdel, at the Lambda Literary Awards in 2007, which were given out for excellence in LGBT literature. I was representing a publisher named Alyson Books, for which I had recently named Executive Editor. Alison had published a couple of graphic novels through Alyson before my arrival, but still, I knew she was a big name on our list. With **FUN HOME**, which she published with a different publisher, it was great to see her reach such new success, and then to watch it transformed into a stage musical was magical.

I worked **FUN HOME** twice. The thing about Circle is, because shows are directed in the round, or sometimes in a horseshoe design where the back end of the seating area is taken up by the stage, it depends where you sit as to what show you see. I saw this show from both main angles, and I heard different things from different characters because of the angle. For sure, **FUN HOME** was a show to see more than once, and not just because of the acoustics in the theatre. Listening to the three actors who played Alison join forces at the end of the show, their soaring voices, the lyrics encompassing the show's theme, well, you would be flying with them.

2018. The most recent show I worked at Circle, as of this writing, was the revival of Ahrens & Flaherty's **ONCE ON THIS ISLAND**. I worked several shifts there, and it was always an interesting experience. Mostly because of the goat. I mean that literally, little lambs. A wildly eclectic set design, such talented actors and singers, that gorgeous score, this was a treat for every sense. During walk-in, as the audience was being seated, one of the actors would bring out to the stage a live goat and those patrons, including the many kids who came to experience the show's beautiful storytelling, would be able to see the live animal up close. It added to the realism of a magical story and set the tone for a lovely night of theatre.

Okay, that's my Circle story for now. I've got two other shows that I've worked longer runs for, **LOMBARDI** and **GODSPELL**. I'll get to those soon. Day by Day I reveal my stories of theatre.

DIARY THIRTY-SEVEN

## I'd Like to Thank the Tony People

This entry comes equipped with a special guest. Not just me, Joseph…but Denzel.

Wait, who? Come on, you know. Like Madonna or Cher, there are few actors, performers or personalities, that can get away with being known by just one name. For proper respect, I'll call him Mr. Washington, but in truth, no one seems to call him that. It's Denzel, and you know what? The theatre patrons love them some Denzel.

I've had a fun history working three of his shows on Broadway, even though I'm sure he has no idea who I am (well, maybe as the empanada man—stay tuned). It's the difference between backstage and front of house that sometimes keeps us all at bay, and that's okay. I respect the boundaries. Heck, I've also worked three shows with Kathleen Turner, and she doesn't know me either (even though I've seen her naked…oh wait, that's another diary…again, stay tuned).

Back to Denzel Washington. Our association began at the Belasco Theatre with **JULIUS CAESAR,** a modern-day take on Shakespeare's classic play. DW was cast in the role of Brutus, but of course he was the headliner and driving force behind the show, which became a sold-out smash hit. I was actually ushering at the Broadhurst Theatre during this time, the run of Billy Crystal's **700 SUNDAYS**. But Billy had taken a week off for vacation after doing his one-man show eight times a week for five months. His needed break meant I got one too. A week off (with pay!).

Um, not so fast.

On the first day of my week off came a call from the Shubert office. They needed ushering assistance that week (lots of theatres had reopened, subs were needed to fill out the house staff) and they told me they knew I had the week off from the Broadhurst. Would I help at another theatre for that week? Two houses were offered to me, so I had a choice in the matter: **MAMMA MIA** at the Winter Garden, or **JULIUS CAESAR** at the Belasco. I mean I could have said no to any work, saying I'd made plans, etc. and so forth, but that's really not my style if it's not true. No is a bad word in our ushering business.

Of course, I didn't even have to think about what theatre I'd choose. ABBA would say "Et tu, Brute?" Yup, I picked **JULIUS CAESAR**, as the Belasco remained one of my favorite theatres to work and it was nice to be reunited with Dexter and the house staff. I would only work the one week, eight shows, at this production, but it gave me more than a hint of Denzel's box office appeal.

It seemed his fans would climb over fences to see him! Ha, a little inside joke. Because the next show I would work in which he starred was a revival of August Wilson's **FENCES**, which won James Earl Jones a Tony Award back during its original run. This time we're at the Cort Theatre (the Belasco was being renovated during this time, so I landed here with thanks to the head usher, William). Also starring Viola Davis, we were a massive hit. To see the balcony at the Cort filled, you knew demand was as high as, well, that balcony and maybe even the roof.

I knew this nightly because the balcony was the section I was assigned to usher, and there was a reason for that. See, I tended to work orchestra or mezz at the Cort, but I'd had a medical mishap and my agility wasn't up for the challenges of those levels, particularly the orchestra. I'd torn the meniscus in my right knee and had required surgery shortly before the start of the run of **FENCES**. I couldn't run up and down the orchestra aisles with the pace needed for such a big hit. *Playbills* in one hand, a cane in the other? Not happening. I took the stairs up to the balcony each performance and just stayed there for the nights when I was on the late shift. Less stress on the healing knee. I remember my physical therapist coming to see the show!

Another memory: we were having a July 4$^{th}$ barbeque in the enclosed alley on the east side of the Cort, everyone attending asked to bring a dish to pass. Near my apartment was a restaurant called Libertador, which made the most amazing empanadas. So, I brought a variety of them, ham & cheese, beef and olives, and the vegetarian choice—good thing I did that last one. While setting out the tray, Denzel walked out and, in that voice of his I knew so well, said, "Who brought the empanadas!" Probably my only interaction with him during the entire run. He chose the veggie one.

Denzel would go on to win the Tony Award for Best Leading Actor for **FENCES**, as would Viola win as Best Leading Actress. The revival itself took the prize for Best Revival of a Play

But I still had one more show on my docket with Denzel. I missed out on his **RAISIN IN THE SUN** at the Barrymore, but a couple years later came Eugene O'Neill's epic **THE ICEMAN COMETH**, which cometh to the Jacobs. I'd been working at the Broadway, a limited run of a show called **ROCKTOPIA** which had just started its limited five-week run. But then I heard about the Jacobs being in need for a second ticket taker. I offered up my services for the 14-week run. I liked to work and this was a longer run, even if it was another O'Neill epic. (4 hours!)

I had a great time at the Jacobs, working with my pal Michael on the doors, and the whole staff there: Michelle, John, Rosa, Martha, Jojo, Yoyo, Carol, the entire gang who welcomed me into their fold for the spring run. I even got to make connections with the local cops, including the mounted police whose van was parked in front of the theatre. One night I jokingly approached one of the horses with my scanner—asking if he had a ticket to the show.

But **ICEMAN** came with its notable challenges. Seven shows a week, earlier curtains than other Broadway productions. We would start at 7:00 pm, 1:00 pm for Saturday matinees, 2:00 pm for Sunday. But here was the caveat for the patrons: don't be late! If they arrived late, people would be escorted down to the lower lobby, where they would sit in chairs and be given infrared listening devices, not to be seated until 8:05, the first intermission. As you can imagine, some people were not pleased that they couldn't be seated. We were just following the late-seat instructions, also the decision of the producers. I tried to placate them by saying Denzel did not appear until 7:55, absent for most of act one.

While Denzel would be nominated for a Tony for his performance in **ICEMAN**, he wouldn't win this time. But if I've learned anything while working his shows, watching his undeniable charm and appeal and big voice, he was stretching his acting chops by taking on these difficult roles, all the while introducing these classics shows to a new generation of patrons. It was pure gold for the producers, grossing over $1,000,000 a week. So, yeah, with that kind of box office pull, he's earned the one-word name: Denzel.

DIARY THIRTY-EIGHT

# Canceled Culture

I must ask this burning question: Do You Really Want to Hurt Me? That would not be good Karma, you colorful Chameleons. Might induce me to sing about how war is stupid. In fact, it might all just be taboo.

Fall 2003, the buzz surrounding the London transfer of Boy George's musical, **TABOO** was palpable. The oversize billboard hovered over Times Square, featuring an unmistakably and unabashed photo promoting the famed British singer, dressed in one of his iconic looks. Broadway uberfan and talk-show host Rosie O'Donnell was producing it single-handedly, taking up residence at the highly coveted Plymouth Theatre on 45th Street. There was lots of press attention for this production, and a giddiness in the air as we entered through the stage door that first night. We were going to be a huge hit—what could go wrong? Sometimes you miss the signs, you miss them blind.

Let's go back a few years (more than a few?) to college. It's 1982 and a new band named Culture Club had burst upon the scene. People didn't know what to think of their lead singer, the flamboyant and smirkingly (is that a word?) androgynous Boy George—birth name George O'Dowd. He took the world by storm, but it wasn't just his outlandish outfits or his outspokenness that united a community, that can only take you so far. The music had to work—and it did.

I was a big fan. I bought the LPs—yup, vinyl —and still own them. Not just the two big ones, *Kissing To Be Clever* and *Colour By Numbers*, but I also have *Waking Up With The House On Fire* and *From Luxury To Heartache*. Even as their fame game began to wane in the late 80s, I was not ready to move away from George. No crying game here.

In one iconic moment of my own, our college newspaper staff was having a big Halloween blowout party, and I arrived dressed in full Boy George regalia. Yes, I have the photo still. I won second prize. But little did I know that my association with this music and this man would make its way into my Broadway life, via London's West End.

**TABOO** began in my favorite city (sorry, NYC). I was there on an extended stay, working on a new novel. I saw lots of shows and one of them had to be the recently opened **TABOO**. During my visit, Boy George himself was co-starring in the show, but not as himself. Instead as the real-life Leigh Bowery, a man of many talents, a man who mixed art and fashion and, in the end, tragedy. This was the role Boy George would reprise on Broadway. I remember sitting inside the small Venue Theatre on the narrow Brewer Street located off Leicester Square, and at one point George as Leigh wanders into the audience. Toying with the patrons, dropping little bon mots as he walked the aisles, he walked past me without giving me a hello. Guess I wasn't cute enough for him to stop, or maybe time wouldn't give him time

But then it was announced that **TABOO** was coming to Broadway. Rosie got lots of press coverage for her daringness to produce her first show on her own. What does Nathan Lane say in **THE PRODUCERS**? Never use your own money. The show was revised for Broadway, with a new book, a rearranging of the order of some songs. Even a couple of the songs from London were dropped and new songs added, including the final number. Check out both CDs. Such great music.

Lots of behind-the-scenes drama was chronicled, much of which was captured by gossip columnist Michael Riedel of the *New York Post*. But Rosie was in the press a lot anyway; she was being sued by a former employee at her magazine. Lots of ink in the NY press and on television, which I think affected ticket sales and the attendance during early previews of the show. It's like the critics were intentionally setting out to slay the show, and boy, did they achieve their goal. Reviews were, uh, mixed.

That didn't stop cast and crew and producer from having a great opening night, complete with a carnival-like atmosphere for the party, with arcade games, face-painting, different vendors serving fun food and drinks. It was indulgent and fun, and no one wanted to leave the festivities, despite the reviews. We knew we were working on something special, even if not everyone got it. **TABOO** was a musical and visual treat, with a dedicated cast who nailed it every night.

Rosie would often come to see the show. At one point, I was informed by the manager that she wanted the ushers to be in full make-up to be more a part of the pre-show action. It would have required us showing up a half hour earlier, which meant overtime pay, but our union put a stop to that idea from what I understand. But I still wore my black **TABOO** show jacket with the logo in red on the back while working the aisles. Its black material stained my white usher shirt to where I had to buy new ones. How many repeat patrons offered to buy the jacket from me is too numerous to count?

**TABOO** wouldn't last, 100 performances only. I remember the Friday after Thanksgiving, usually one of the busiest nights on Broadway, when some wag said, "Even **TABOO** is sold out." We had a rocky run. But a fun one. The talent on that stage was unmatched. From Euan Morton's lush voice as Boy George for "Stranger in this World," to Raul Esparza's chilling "Petrified," to Liz McCartney's soaring anthem "Talk Amongst Yourselves." When in the audience, Rosie would stand up and wave her arms when Liz's voice rose (rosied?) to that big climactic note of that song.

We'd close Feb 8, 2004, a mere 4 months from opening. A more subdued party occurred at the late-and-lamented Barrymore's, found just down 45th Street. Just the entire gang, saying our final goodbyes. But that last night holds one more memory for me. I was relieving the ticket taker in the Plymouth's lobby during Act II, my usual duty when on the late shift. A devoted crowd was hanging out in front of the theatre. They'd been unable to secure tickets to the final performance. Rosie came to me and asked if we could let them in. Now, I don't have that kind of authority (but it was nice she thought I did!), so I checked with the house manager about what the procedure was. We ended up lining those fans up right inside against Aisle 1 in the orchestra, and they got to hear the final, stirring notes of a song called, appropriately, "Come on In from the Outside."

**TABOO**, we hardly knew you, but we loved you. ("We love you George," as one actress ad-libbed during the end of the first act.) Both in London and in NYC, to paraphrase the cast, you were never out of fashion.

DIARY THIRTY-NINE

## Um, it's JOHN Wilkes Booth

Let's get a little intimate now, and by that word I mean a visit to one off the smaller theatres on Broadway, and one that has a storied history of many hits. We're talking The Booth Theatre.

For years, the Booth remained elusive to me; the office just never sent me there for work, but in truth I usually had steady work, oftentimes at the other theatres on West 45$^{th}$ Street nearby. At only 766 seats, it's the smallest of the Shubert-owned houses, which means they require a fewer number of ushers. It's a beautiful theatre, built in 1910, named after the famed 19$^{th}$ century actor, Edwin Booth. (Not his infamous brother; more on that later, too, and it's good for a laugh.)

The first show I ever watched at the Booth was **OUR TOWN**, starring Paul Newman as the narrator. Since I was in a production of this play during my junior year of high school, Thornton Wilder's classic held a special place in my heart. I loved hearing, again those lines I knew so well, smiling as I watched my role, paperboy Joe Crowell tossing the morning newspaper onto those imaginary stoops. It was typecasting; there was a time this Joe held down two paper routes! But not on Broadway.

The first show I ever worked at the Booth Theatre was the revival of Lily's Tomlin's **THE SEARCH FOR SIGNS OF INTELLIGENT LIFE IN THE UNIVERSE**. I had a rare Sunday off from **JEKYLL & HYDE**, so I picked up an extra shift, finally making my Booth debut. But after that, that building returned to its previous status as a theatre I walked past en route to the Plymouth or the Royale or the Golden, all of which I'd worked multiple times. Until...

During the 2010s decade, I started doing this extra gig for the Shubert Organization, with the office notifying me of the need for a second ticket taker for opening nights at various houses. My contact there, Mary, knew I loved working those special nights, crazy and busy as they can be, so I got booked at the Booth for the opening of **THE ELEPHANT MAN** starring Bradley Cooper and Patricia Clarkson. I only got to see some of the show, since my job entailed monitoring the lobby and trying to keep the paparazzi quiet. I did get to attend the after party.

Here's a fun story about that late night. I went to the party venue, a fancy former bank now turned into a banquet hall named Gotham. Accompanying the regular house staff at the Booth, we had such a great time eating and drinking and chatting; we had to be among the last to be kicked out when the party ended. We weren't alone in being late departures. The co-star, Ms. Clarkson and her entourage were in the same boat, and suddenly we found both of ours factions walking up 7$^{th}$ Avenue at midnight, all of us knowing the party might be over at Gotham, but the night was still young. I was actually talking with Ms. Clarkson, she in her party gown, me in my ticket-taker suit. "Where you going?" "Some hotel bar." "We're going to an Irish pub." That was pretty much our exchange. It was a Sunday night and I bet that Hilton bar on 42$^{nd}$ Street she'd referenced was already closed. O'Donoghue's on 44$^{th}$ Street was still open.

The lesson: trust the house staff. We know where and when to go.

A coda to this story. About a year later, Steve took me for my birthday to Joe's Pub in the Village for a Betty Buckley concert. She's one of his all-time favorites. It was great, but between songs Betty mentioned a few special guests in the audience, including Ms. Clarkson. Steve, a huge fan of her, too, did a big gasp. Well, at the end of the show, I put on my best "ticket taker" persona and approached her. I mentioned how I had been her TT for **THE ELEPHANT MAN** and that my (at the time boyfriend, now husband) was a huge fan of hers. Cut to: a photo op. She was very gracious about my lack of being able to take a good photo with my phone.

Okay, back to the Booth for other adventures and shows. My next opening night there was a play called **AMERICAN SON**, starring Kerry Washington and Steven

Pasquale. Again, I was only able to see part of the show, but also, again, I did get to enjoy the after party—same venue of Gotham. I was getting comfortable hanging with the Booth (and Gotham), and that would increase exponentially.

Next up, a revival of the iconic gay play, **THE BOYS IN THE BAND**. While I didn't get opening night there, I received an emergency text one Monday afternoon, the manager needed a ticket taker. That night. I hopped the train and was there for this all-star production. Again, I missed a lot of the show given my duties in the lobby. But I was called for another shift a couple of weeks later, this time as an usher, and got to watch Jim Parsons (Sheldon!), Zachary Quinto (Spock!), Matt Bomer, Tuc Watkins (from "One Life to Live") and others in this ground-breaking work.

And now we've come to my final Booth Theatre story. I was asked by the office to be the second ticket taker in 2019 for the run of the hip-hop improv show co-produced by Lin-Manuel Miranda, **FREESTYLE LOVE SUPREME**. For those three months I was there for every show, working with such a great staff. Joann, Nicole, Bernadette, Marjorie, Marco, Chrissy, Phil, Nadine, Daniel, they welcomed me and made me feel part of the Booth family. Sarah and Jacob at merch were kinda cool, too! And Jonathan and the gang at the bar.

Here's an amusing aside about my experience there during this run. We had a staff meeting between shows with our customer service advisor, sandwiches and salad provided by the office. It was just a tutorial on the ever-changing way of greeting our customers, an informative exchange between executives and those of us in the field. Except when we were given a lesson in the history of the theatre, including being reminded of its namesake, Edwin. Not his brother, "James Wilkes Booth," as it was stated. It took all my teeth to bite my tongue and not cry out, "It's JOHN."

But for a theatre that eluded me for all so many years, it became a new favorite of mine in which to work. I'd go back anytime.

## DIARY FORTY

# A Strange Show Just Passing Through

I'm calling this entry, in true "Friends" style, "The One that Begins the Belasco Trilogy, and given my history with this beautiful theatre it's not going to be the last time we'll enter its doors. But for now, these three linked stories, to be unfolded in the next series of chapters, are held by a particular time period: it encompasses a closing, a reopening, and as it turned out, a couple of passings. I'm writing here now about the last two shows to play the Belasco before the stunning renovation done to the theatre in 2009-2010, and then I'll finally write about the show that reopened it and all the emotions wrapped around such an event.

Let's begin. It's February 2008 when I made my return (again) to the Belasco, this time for the run of an unlikely musical for Broadway: the rock show **PASSING STRANGE**. Written by a musician named Stew, narrated by him on stage with his band (and co-author Heidi Rodewald), this coming-of-age story took audiences from the black churches of LA to the Red-Light district of Amsterdam, with a few interesting stops along the way.

With a great cast, including Daniel Breaker, Colman Domingo, Rebecca Naomi Jones, Eisa Davis, Chad Goodridge, and De'Adre Aziza, **PASSING STRANGE** was fresh, exciting and during one point in the show, so loud and rollicking I thought the ceiling of our 1907-built house might not survive. Called "Keys (It's Alright)," the song came near the end of Act I, one of the most electrifying moments I'd ever seen on a stage. The lighting sold it: bright, colorful, and blinding. The energy on that stage infused with Stew's power chords on the guitar shocked the audience. The house staff, ushers and porters and cleaners and box office and ticket taker, used to rock out at the back of the theatre for that song every night. Caroline, Monica, Kitty, Pamela, we had such fun dancing behind the back row.

**PASSING STRANGE** would receive great reviews after opening night on February 25, but it struggled to find a traditional Broadway audience. Thankfully the Tony nominators loved the show's uniqueness, power, and energy (reportedly Mr. Schoenfeld, head of the theatre's owner, The Shubert Organization, loved it, too). **PS** would garner seven Tony nominations, including one for Best Musical. It would only win one Tony though that June: for Stew, receiving the Best Book of a Musical award. That was also the year the buzzy **IN THE HEIGHTS** premiered, so there you go. Lin-Manuel

Miranda became a household name. Stew, not so much.

Two stories to recount from during the run of the production. First, the original cast album was being recorded live on the Belasco stage, an invited audience filling the house. The manager needed some staff to help work the front of the house, so I signed up. Whenever I listen to the cast recording, I imagine I can hear my hollers and applause. As it was just a recording, the entire cast was on stage seated on bar stools, holding their microphones; no need to do the staged production in full. This was about the words and the music.

As opposed to what happened the final weekend of **PASSING STRANGE**'s Broadway run. Spike Lee had agreed to direct the live show, the filming spread out over a couple nights. There is a DVD of the show available at retail outlets; no bootleg, this. You can pop in the disc to experience Stew's stirring rock vision and the spectacular cast, all set amidst Spike Lee's interpretation of that unique story. I had to watch the movie, because I couldn't be there for the filming. I'd been in Italy at one of my best friends' destination wedding (I know, poor me…), so I had to take vacation time during this time. Our closing notice for **PASSING STRANGE** came abruptly, for July, same week that I was traveling for the wedding. Obviously, there was nothing I could do; can't be in two places at one time. But in truth, I couldn't not not be in Italy; after all, I was in the wedding party, one of only four people standing up for our friends.

The celebration was in Arezzo at a private villa with so many bedrooms and a pool that overlooked the rolling hills, the fields of sunflowers abundant rolling across the scenic Tuscany valley. A far cry from the crumbling Belasco on West 44th Street in New York City.

Except, hmm, maybe there was a way I could maybe figure out how to have my wedding cake and eat it too. I was scheduled to be back in the city by Friday of that week of the filming of **PASSING STRANGE**, so I could have worked those three weekend shifts with no problem.

Enter: problem. The office said no, not if I couldn't work the entire week. (That was a rule of theirs, though rarely enforced. I'll admit that I was disappointed by such a decision). Instead, I accepted three shifts at **BOEING BOEING** at the Longacre starring Mark Rylance and Christine Baranski, all while knowing that the Belasco must be buzzing with excitement blocks away. Later, when the Belasco's house manager heard I had been available to work that weekend, she expressed how unhappy she was at the office's decision. She said she would have spoken with her bosses, saying for such an event as Spike Lee filming the show, she wanted her regular staff patrolling the aisles I worked center orchestra, a busy aisle.

Sometimes corporate makes dumb decisions. This was one of them.

But let's move on.

Yeah, not all of my memories of working these theatres comes with a happy ending, but when they don't they instead invoke their own pathos. Those situations make memories as much as do the great ones. My life is a series of hits of flops.

**PASSING STRANGE** closed that Sunday in July without me. That passing, was, uh, can I say it? Strange.

But my return to the Belasco would continue with our next show, but I'm going to save that for the next chapter. It deserves its proper due. I think it's worth it, an important piece of history in both this theatre and on Broadway itself. Given my tendency of coming and going at the Belasco over the past two decades, I jokingly referred to our upcoming show as "Joe Pittman's Come and Gone." Ha! But of course, it's called **JOE TURNER'S COME AND GONE**, one of August Wilson's acclaimed plays.

I should title this upcoming chapter as "Mr. President Comes to Broadway," but as you'll see, I took a more personal approach to the chapter title, because something, and someone, would soon be gone.

## DIARY FORTY-ONE

# The Balcony is Closed

In 1907, David Belasco built his dream theatre, on West 44$^{th}$ Street near the corner of 6$^{th}$ Avenue. It would end up being the eastern-most Broadway house in the neighborhood, and as someone who lived in an apartment on the Upper East Side, it was a convenient location for me. But I loved that creaky old house —with the old-fashioned telephone booth situated outside the men's room and the original usher's room, which once housed a swimming pool —for more reasons than a quicker commute home at night.

The Belasco, I've stated, was a bit rundown, with rumors of its closing down for a long-needed renovation coming to fruition. A reclamation project was in the works and because of that truth, the theatre sought a final new booking until the date of its closure had been decided upon. But, our little-theatre-that could finally announced a date for July of 2009. It would be closed for 18 months.

But not before one more show would take its stage.

It's March of 2009, and August Wilson's celebrated play **JOE TURNER'S COME AND GONE** took up residence for a 14-week limited run. Wilson wrote 10 plays, often referred to as The Century Cycle, or The Pittsburgh Cycle, chronicling the lives of black people over the course of each decade of the 20$^{th}$ Century. An ambitious project, a concept I admired as a writer myself. He achieved his goal before his death, and in honor of his achievement Jujamcyn Theatres renamed their Virginia Theatre, now known as the August Wilson Theatre. The highest honor on Broadway is to have a marquee bearing your name. Most are done, though, posthumously.

**JOE TURNER** was a production that came from Lincoln Center Theater, which often used Shubert-owned houses for their shows when their own Broadway theatre, the Vivian Beaumont, was already booked. Mr. Gersten and Mr. Bishop, the executives at LCT seemed to like the Belasco (more on LCT in the following chapter). **JOE TURNER** also holds the distinction as being the only August Wilson play to date, original or revival, directed by a non-African-American. LCT resident director Bartlett Sher was given special permission by the Wilson estate from what I read.

The show opened on April 16, 2009. It didn't have a "star" in the cast, rather a collection of stage veterans, some of Wilson's favorites, and one Ghostbuster. Among the cast was LaTanya Richardson Jackson (wife of Samuel L.), eventual Tony-winner for this show Roger

Robinson, and the aforementioned buster of ghosts, Ernie Hudson.

**JT**, as I shortened it, opened to great reviews and received six Tony nominations. But were we a hit? Uh, not exactly. While LCT productions are subscription-based, it's still a commercial venture being at the Belasco. We needed some press, and press is what we would eventually get. In the form of President Barack Obama himself. Yup, this was the show he famously brought First Lady Michelle too, his so-called "date night" he'd promised her after winning the election.

Before I get to that night, let me tell you about my feelings on the Belasco. The whole staff knew that when this show closed, the theatre would remain dark for a while, as it was scheduled, finally, for its destined renovation. We would all have to part ways, find work at other theatres for the duration of the shutdown. (I did, both at the Lyceum and the Cort—I guess I specialize in those east of Broadway houses!). I remember looking around at the house, at the seats, the curtains, the little door the staff used to climb through to gain access to the balcony. It was all going to change. I loved my Belasco as it was, but also knew that these changes were inevitable. What would it look like? Fortune favored its future.

The fortunes of **JOE TURNER** were about to change too. Something was up, a buzz in the air. The staff were informed one night that a very special VIP would be attending a performance of the show on a Saturday night in June—just two weeks shy of our announced closing. Yes, the new president of the United States was coming to Broadway. It was scheduled for the upcoming that coming weekend night, an 8:00 pm curtain.

But the story of POTUS's visit starts the night before. An intrepid photographer who had received advance word of Obama's visit had bought a ticket for the Friday night performance. At the end of the show, as we were clearing the house of the audience, I noticed this man was taking photographs of the stage, of the seats, of the entire theatre really, which back then was prohibited on any normal night. But this night, knowing what was happening the next day, well, I alerted the house manager to this activity, and she alerted house security to the breach in protocol. The photographer in question protested that he had a right to take the photos, but it was finally a Secret Service advance man, already on duty, who put the kibosh on the man's actions. They took away his film.

Cut to the next day, that Saturday matinee. I was working the balcony door during the run of this show, a separate entrance just down the street from the main house doors. A woman came by and said to me, "Well, you have an exciting day today," then claiming the President was coming to see our show, she'd read about it that morning in the *Daily News*. I couldn't acknowledge it or deny it, as we'd all been instructed to not say anything. Again, a security issue.

I just said to her, "You know more than me."

But already the excitement was building in the building all afternoon.

Cut to Saturday night. I'm on the steps of the balcony entrance with our house security and a Secret Service agent as we readied to open the house. I saw the motorcade turning off Sixth Avenue onto 44th Street—the street was blocked off and so they were allowed to drive the wrong way on a one-way. I watched as two limousines pulled up to the Belasco's entrance and I saw two people emerge from the first of those cars. No, it's not them but believed to be their body doubles, meant as a distraction. And then emerged from the second limousine, Barack and Michelle.

I remember taking a step down to grab a look and feel the excitement in the air. The Secret Service agent told me, in such an authoritative voice, to resume my post back up on the stairs. Yes, Ma'am. This was serious business, but it was a thrilling moment, nonetheless. All of 44th Street was blocked off in both directions, but still crowds gathered at the barricades at each end, and you could hear the people cheering their president and his wife.

That night, the 8:00 pm show didn't go up until 8:45 and as I was on the late shift, I made some overtime pay. Thanks, Prez.

The Obama's seeing the show gave **JOE TURNER'S COME AND GONE** a huge boost at the box office. We were sold out for the final two weeks of the run, not a seat to be had—even in that lamented balcony. There was no chance of an extension, the wheels of the renovation were in full roll out and I guess the actors had other commitments.

Final thoughts on **JOE TURNER** and the Belasco itself: for the house staff, we were sad on that final performance day, a Sunday matinee. We took pictures, and again we gazed around at a theatre that appropriately once housed a revival of **FOLLIES**. Yes, ghosts were ever-present that day, the artwork on the walls faded, the Tiffany-glass ceiling coated with years of grime. David himself no doubt sitting in his box, aware of the history occurring on this day. I remember going to my balcony door for one last time, having a picture taken of me for posterity. It's an honor to know I am the last person to ever work that balcony door.

The Obamas sat in Orchestra row K, on the aisle, seats 101-102. Close enough to have a great view of the show but protected from any sudden security issue by the mezzanine overhang. The week after we closed, as the renovation process began and the old seats were being placed in a dumpster, an intrepid usher named Chris asked for the Obama seats as they were being thrown out. He got them and ended up selling them on eBay. Only in New York kids, only in New York. **JOE TURNER** had truly come and gone, and so had the Obamas.

I'd be back to the Belasco. It would just take a while.

DIARY FORTY-TWO

# A Reopening While on the Verge of Tears

In this final chapter of the so-called "The Belasco Trilogy," we uncover a tale of redemption, revival, and renewal. It's also the story of the new musical, **WOMEN ON THE VERGE OF A NERVOUS BREAKDOWN**, the first show to reopen the newly renovated, and stunning, Belasco Theatre. The date is October 8, 2010. After 18 months of being closed, it's long-awaited return is happening, and guess what? I'm not there.

Life works in mysterious, incongruous ways, leaving certain memories seared in your mind forever. For a year-and-a-half the staff at the Belasco was scattered to the winds (wings?) of other theatres while the extensive renovation was underway. I was given a spot at the Lyceum initially, working the play, another LCT production, **IN THE NEXT ROOM** (or The Vibrator Play), then at the Cort for **A VIEW FROM THE BRIDGE** starring Liev Schreiber and Scarlett Johansson, and then **FENCES** with Denzel. The final show I'd work at the Cort before returning to the Belasco was **TIME STANDS STILL** with Laura Linney, in the Fall of 2010.

Time was not standing still, though. The Belasco's scheduled opening kept getting delayed, the show still not ready for audiences and so we waited a couple of weeks for a new date. But one day I was walking past the Belasco in early September, after attending a celebration of the life for an usher and friend who had passed. I checked in to say hi to the box office staff and simply asked how the theatre looked. They said why not take a look for yourself. And then buzzed me in through the front access door.

I took a long, deep breath. So much history here beyond this door. So much anticipation of what had been, what was to be. I closed my eyes, and then set them alight. I'd walked these aisles for so many shows and for so many years, feeling like I'd grown up within these walls. But what I saw before me on this day was…the rediscovery of a Broadway treasure. New seats, new curtains, sure, I expected that. But all the faded artwork on the walls had been restored, vibrant and bright amidst the new lighting that pierced the house with its fresh glow. The old light fixtures underneath the mezzanine overhang were back, no longer just exposed light bulbs I was used to seeing reflect off the shiny covers of my stack of *Playbills*.

But the true visual treat was the vaulted ceiling. I stared, and I stared some more. Beauty sinking into me. The original Tiffany glass had been restored and cleaned and oh, combined with the other features that had a new gleam to them, it was a sight to behold. I was so thrilled to stand in the center orchestra section and just look up, all by myself, being given the privilege of a private audience within this palace. Just me, the theatre, and maybe Belasco's ghost roamed the aisles and levels on that afternoon. I'm sure he loved what they did with his theatrical child.

Then there were the other changes that had been made to the theatre: while the Alice closet remained, it was no longer our access door to the balcony. That didn't exist anymore. Instead, the stairs leading up to the mezzanine now included a new staircase located on house right that led to the balcony. All three levels were now incorporated and accessible through the main entrance. As someone who started ushering in that balcony, this redo was a revelation. I couldn't wait to return for our first preview and watch the reaction of the staff and the crowd to this theatrical treasure.

Again, that return would need to wait. There were more important things going on than the reopening of the Belasco's doors. Yes, **WOMEN ON THE VERGE** had finally announced their new start day for its first preview. But a few hours away from the Great White Way, a twinkling set of eyes were getting set to close for the last time. My father, Gerard, passed on the night of October 8, 2010, the same day of the first preview of **WOMEN ON**

**THE VERGE.** It was 7:18 pm, twelve minutes before the new manager would say, "the house is open." It was a strange dichotomy that still haunts me and will forever. How can a reopening and a passing happen within minutes of each other?

I wouldn't return to the Belasco for 10 days, as I was obviously taking care of family issues first. But it always struck me as a sign of both remembrance and renewal, history and future, losing my father and regaining the walls of the Belasco. During the months leading up to the reopening, I'd been promoted to the position of "director," which meant I greeted people on the orchestra level and helped get them to their proper aisles where their usher would then assist them with the final step of taking their seat. I wanted to return. But my mom needed me first.

Now, what about the show itself, what was happening while I was away? **WOMEN ON THE VERGE OF A NERVOUS BREAKDOWN** was a musical based on the acclaimed Pedro Almodovar film. Produced by Lincoln Center Theater (yup, they were back at the Belasco), it had the most awesome cast you could imagine for a Broadway musical: Brian Stokes Mitchell, Patti Lupone, Laura Benanti, Sherie Rene Scott, Danny Burstein, among others. With a score by David Yazbek (**THE FULL MONTY, DIRTY ROTTEN SCOUNDRELS**) and Bartlett Sher once again directing, what could go wrong?

Lots. To put it plainly, **WOTVOANB** (how's that for an

acronym?) was just not ready for prime time. Changes were made continually throughout the preview process, including moving the Act II opener to actually open Act I—the taxicab scene with Danny sporting a blonde wig which introduced all the zany characters and situations. There was a scene later in Act I where Sherie's character burns a bed on stage, and the smoke from it stunk up the house to the point where patrons complained of the odor at intermission. Laura was great; her "Model Behavior" song was a study in comedic timing and the audience devoured it. You could tell she was having fun.

The critics weren't having as much fun when the show opened on November 4, 2010. No opening night party for the house staff, we weren't invited, but I didn't expect to be. LCT wasn't the friendliest in that regard toward including front of house. But a bunch of us went across the street to the Long Room gastropub and raised a glass (or two) in knowing our beautiful theatre was back up and running. I might have raised my glass a little higher, up toward heaven.

**WOMEN ON THE VERGE** had been announced as a limited run, one that became more limited than we expected. We closed two weeks earlier than scheduled, the first week of January 2011. I remember we had a performance on New Year's Day, and as I'm entering through the stage door entrance, who is doing so at the same time? Ms. Lupone. She was the first person to wish me a Happy New Year in 2011. That's good company.

The show shut down early, as I've heard, because they wanted to save the production costs so the producers and composer could record the cast album. They did, and it's really fun to listen to, conjuring memories in my mind that go beyond the show itself. Yeah, it was an imperfect show, even with its stellar cast, but what I most take away from **WOMEN ON THE VERGE OF A NERVOUS BREAKDOWN** is that sense of life it gave to me. You miss what you can no longer have, but you honor that by being who you can be.

The Belasco remains today as the most beautiful theatre on Broadway.

DIARY FORTY-THREE

# I'll Have What He's Having

Here's the story of an usher named Joseph and an actor named Billy and how their worlds collided for what seemed like, well, 700 nights. Let us both explain, as we explore the world that was Billy Crystal's one-man smash-hit show, **700 SUNDAYS**, which played an extended run at the 1,156-seat Broadhurst Theatre.

I'm JP, he's BC.

JP: Hey, thanks for agreeing to do this. What do you say, let's reminisce about the show in a Q&A format, that ok with you?

BC: Is that the first question?

JP: Ha. You're a funny guy. But you're also a heartfelt guy, based on your autobiographical play that detailed the "700 Sundays" you spent with your father, before losing him when you were 15. Writing your story must have brought up lots of pain and childhood issues, and then performing it in front of an adoring crowd, was no doubt a mix of reward and regret. But you also shared a lot of history about famous people, and of a time during your formative years and what experiences and emotions helped shaped the man you became. It was very moving. But it was also a long show.

BC: And it kept getting longer.

JP: Yeah, that much I remember. It started at two hours and thirty minutes and by the time of the final curtain on June 12, 2005, it was three hours and fifteen minutes. I remember patrons each night asking me how long the show lasted, and I'd tell them it depends on Billy, but plan on three hours. They always seemed surprised at the length for a only a one-man show. That took stamina! Why the changing end times?

BC: I had more things to say.

JP: Apparently. Anyway, I didn't come to work your show until January of 2005, even though you opened in December—appropriately, on a Sunday. See, I was working up at the Broadway Theatre, finishing up the run of London-import **BOMBAY DREAMS** and so was looking for my next gig. Well, the Shubert Organization holds an annual holiday party at Sardis (I love that almost-rhyme) every year and I happened to run into the head usher from the Broadhurst, Roseanne. She invited me to join the staff for the run of your show and so that's how I ended up there.

BC: That's a long explanation. I guess you had more things to say, too.

JP: LOL. Anyway, moving on. Your show wasn't the

easiest one to work. First of all, there were a lot of rules for us ushers. We only got a ten-minute break in each act, and for the rest of the time we were required to stand at the back of the house, managing people who got up during the show to use the restrooms. We also had to deal with those same patrons who thought the show was over before it was over. Did you realize you had this moment, about 10 minutes before the end where you stood, crossed your arms and smiled as though "that's it." The audience would start to applause and many even got up to leave before the curtain call. But then you went into your epilogue.

BC: It just seemed the right directional choice. Or maybe my B&T audience just had a train to catch.

JP: I know the feeling now. I'm a Jersey Boy now.

BC: I'm sorry.

(We both laughed at that one.)

JP: By the way, your sold-out audience every night was entirely focused on you and your story. They loved the one about how you sat on Billie Holiday's lap as a kid in a movie theatre; I believe it was the first movie you saw. You certainly met some interesting people through your uncle's shop, Commodore Records.

BC: I did, and thanks for remembering that. Memories like that enhanced and gave further shape to the story I was telling. Time and place were important to me. But in the end, my tale always wrapped around that porch and my father and our history and yup, that house on Long Island.

JP: Yes, the set was modeled after the house you grew up in. That must have been surreal, but for the audience it gave credence, reality, to the show. They knew what they were witnessing was real and honest. I could tell, I mean, I saw the show nightly for six months!

BC: Uh, I gave you a week off in March. With pay. We all had a vacation.

JP: Speaking of vacations, I had one planned for June, right after your final performance. I was going to Italy, Rome specifically, and I'll tell you that the tips I earned on Aisle 4 in the orchestra helped give me some spending liras. (I guess it was the Euro by then.). See, I was also responsible for bringing patrons up to the box seats, and I would draw the curtain open and announce to them it was their private arena for the night. They slipped me some bucks.

BC: Did I get a commission from them?

JP: Uh, no, but you look mahvelous.

BC: I was waiting for that.

JP: Anyway, those tips were saved in an envelope in anticipation of the Italy trip. I bought my Dad a rosary from the Vatican with some of that cash. I also sent a postcard to my parents, a picture of the Colosseum with the message that I bet you would have sold out that place, too!

BC: You sure have a lot of memories of working my show. For me, I got to have it filmed by HBO, then turned into a book, and I brought the show back for the holidays in 2013, this time playing the Imperial Theatre. Well, this has been a fun walk down Broadway, but I gotta run.

JP: Me too. I've got more tales to tell about my life on Broadway. And in fact, you've inspired me on what the next chapter I'll focus on. One of my favorites: the Imperial awaits. Thanks for this, Billy, see you at **MR. SATURDAY NIGHT.**

BC: What can I say, I like weekends.

P.S. I wrote all of these exchanges and Mr. Crystal did not participate. I hope he doesn't mind my attempt at parody, my fun way to honor the experience of working his show.

DIARY FORTY-FOUR

## War, Told in Pieces

The Imperial Theatre is one of the most desired musical houses, a history that includes the original productions of **CABARET** (one of its many stops during is run), **DREAMGIRLS, OLIVER!**, and the short-lived but ABBA-esque **CHESS**. Oh, of course, **LES MISERABLES**—a plaque is placed before the front entrance honoring its legendary run. But then came a new show that told a bit of war, a bit of peace. Glad you're here, but you know who's not? Andrey. If you know that reference, I'll toss you a box of perogies. Need more info? Read on.

As the opening song says, "Natasha is young. Sonya is good. Mayra is old school. Anatole is hot. Helene is a slut. Dolokhov is fierce. Old Prince Bokonsky is crazy. Mary is in pain. And Balaga's just for fun.

"But what about Pierre?"

Yes, it's time to delve into the fascinating world of **NATASHA, PIERRE & THE GREAT COMET OF 1812**, one of the most exhilarating experiences I've ever had working on Broadway. The year was 2017 (for me, not the setting of the show!), **FIDDLER ON THE ROOF** had just closed at the Broadway Theatre and I was invited to join the staff of the Imperial for three months until we reopened in March with the revival of **MISS SAIGON.**

I'd actually already worked **COMET** once, the previous December, while filling in on a rare matinee off. I'd heard awesome reviews of the show, of the design, so I was eager to see what the set designer had done with the Imperial. As I walked through the lobby door I was amazed and excited by the creatively, the vibrancy, abounding in the aisles and on the stage. The theatre had been completely transformed into a Russian salon, seating on the stage and cast members running around the house during the performance. That afternoon I was asked to do the stage seating, which required that I remain up there during the show, sitting in a chair behind the last row. It gave me a unique perspective, not only of the show, but of the theatre. I'd only ever faced the stage. But in truth, I felt claustrophobic up there.

When I arrived in January, with a couple of my Broadway coworkers in tow, I asked that I not be assigned up there if possible. Instead, I was assigned to Orchestra Aisle 2, down front. Which meant I had to do not only the traditional seating, but some of the tables at the edge of the stage and up on the lip of the stage. This was more to my liking. But it was complicated seating, and each usher was given a map of all the seat locations, just to make sure we all knew our sections. There were cocktail tables, each marked starting with the letter A. I think we went all the way to the letter T.

Now let's talk about the show itself. What a blast from start to finish. The cast was all over that theatre, and we ushers had to stay out of their way—we were practically hugging the back walls as numerous characters ran through the back of the house and flooded the aisles. First of all, handing out the fresh-made perogies was a real thing—a local bakery provided them and the cast would toss small boxes of them to audience members during the show's prologue. Just a way to get them in a Russian mood.

**GREAT COMET** has a complicated plot, but the opening number, as slightly quoted at the start of my diary, did a good job of introducing all (read: many) characters. Probably better than Tolstoy did! Each actor owned their role, and among my favorites were Amber Gray as Helene, Lucas Steele as Anatole, and Denee Benton as Natasha.

But what about Pierre? The incomparable (and I don't use that word lightly) Josh Groban played the role, and to hear that voice nightly was a lovely bonus. From his Act I balled "Dust and Ashes" to the quiet, anthemic closing number, "The Great Comet of 1812," it was like liquid gold slipping into your ears. His character enriched the action and gave the show its moral center, all while craziness was erupting around him.

It was just such a joy to be a part of this ground-breaking work by creator Dave Malloy. He wrote the whole thing: music, lyrics, book. An impressive, sung-through achievement of taking one small section of Leo Tolstoy's classic, dense novel and, under the masterful direction of Rachel Chavkin, they turned a tough subject into a once-in-a-lifetime show. The Imperial had done that before, when hosting Victor Hugo's epic **LES MISERABLES**.

And everyone I knew wanted to see it! Once friends and family found out I was working there, requests flooded in for tickets. The box office and I had made friends when I worked **LES MIZ** there as a ticket taker, and so they helped me secure those table seats, set near the stage bars down front. Kudos to them, and also huge thanks to the entire Imperial house staff for welcoming me back, but a special shout out to my partner in perogies, Joanna. She and I worked Aisle 2 like a well-oiled machine. And who could forget that the bar staff created an "Anadoll," who stood guard over them as they served up specialty drinks. Well done, Kristen and Jonathan.

I was also asked to be the back-up ticket taker when one of their regular two took a night off, so that was also a plus to be in the lobby. But when you were working in the house, the antics on that stage and all over the house were so thrilling to watch, your curious eyes darted all about, never knowing where to look. Except in that final moment, that "firmament," as Pierre sang, that gave the show its ultimate glow.

I would watch that glorious song on my every late shift, listening for the soft, chill-inducing background vocals coming from the rest of the cast. But Josh filled that song, that moment, with such emotion, accompanied by a talented band of musicians.

I can still see that comet at it descended when I close my eyes, still feel it when I play the cast album.

**GREAT COMET** opened on November 14, 2016 and closed on September 3, 2017, amidst a casting controversy I thought the show didn't deserve. It fell victim to gossip and media scrutiny, and the message of the recasting of Pierre got lost. I was sad to see it close, to realize all those people were suddenly unexpectedly, out of work. Even though I'd moved back to the Broadway Theatre at that point, **COMET** still remains an indelible part of my Broadway history.

And yes, finally, Andrey was there.

## DIARY FORTY-FIVE

# You'd Like to Win a Tony?

I ran into an old friend and one-time head usher at the Plymouth Theatre recently, and our exchange conjured images, thoughts and experiences of the shows I'd worked at that house. I've previously detailed a few of those in earlier diaries: **JEKYLL & HYDE, TABOO, LONG DAY'S JOURNEY INTO NIGHT**. But there were others, before and after those shows. It was my regular house for six years and I'd also filled in at other times during my career.

The Plymouth, now called the Gerald Schoenfeld Theatre after the late Shubert chairman, is one of the most coveted houses on Broadway. It's 1,080 seats is ideal for both a play or a smaller-scaled musical. Barely a bad seat in the house, and now, after it's renovation, offers more suitable space and access for the patrons who might need...um, a bathroom. Getting to the facilities at the Plymouth when I worked there was an intermission nightmare.

The first play, well, playing at the Plymouth when I first started ushering for the Shubert Organization was Brian Friel's **DANCING AT LUGHNASA**, a big Tony-winner in 1992. I had friends who worked there and on some Saturday nights a bunch of us would meet up after our respective shows and go out for late-night drinks. Me from the Belasco, Michael from the Majestic. An ecumenical Broadway night out.

But the Plymouth already had a rich history of hits and award-winning shows way before **LUGHNASA**—the original production of **THE HEIDI CHRONICLES**, **THE SEARCH FOR SIGNS OF INTELLIGENCE LIFE IN THE UNIVERSE, THE REAL THING,** which won Tonys for the playwright, the director Mike Nichols, and stars Jeremy Irons, Glenn Close, and Christine Baranski. The famed epic **NICHOLAS NICKELBY** played the Plymouth, too, again, taking home multiple Tonys. (Starring the late Roger Rees, who I knew as Robin Colcord on "Cheers.) Go back in time and what you'll see is a cavalcade of stars and awards playing that stage.

The Plymouth is a hit maker. But like most theatres, it's had its missteps.

The first show I worked at the Plymouth was Stephen Sondheim's **PASSION**—yup, winner of Best Musical at the Tonys, and a win, too, for Donna Murphy in her acclaimed performance as Fosca. I was assigned there for the final three months of the show's short run. It wasn't a big hit, either with audiences or with some critics. But my biggest takeaway from watching this production was being introduced to the powerful voice and presence of Marin Mazzie, who ended up starring in my most favorite musical ever, Ahrens and Flaherty's **RAGTIME**. Her "Back to Before" in that latter show is a stunning Act II showstopper. How Broadway misses her.

Then came **TRANSLATIONS**, another Brian Friel play, trying to build on the success of **LUGHNASA**. It didn't work. The show lasted only seven weeks, despite its starry cast. My first time ever seeing Brian Dennehy live (who would later win a Tony on that same stage for **LONG DAY'S JOURNEY INTO NIGHT**), and of course I had a huge crush on Dana Delaney of "China Beach" fame, and then some unknown guy (at the time) named Rufus Sewell was featured. It was a drama that was unfortunately played for too many laughs.

Despite being asked to transfer full-time to the Plymouth Susie, the head usher, I knew the show wouldn't last and I was scheduled to return to my regular position at the Barrymore Theatre in a matter of weeks. I liked to work and enjoyed my center orchestra aisle at the Barrymore.

My time, though, with this legendary theatre was far from over.

A rare matinee off, I grabbed an extra shift over at the Plymouth for the LCT revival of Edward Albee's tense **A DELICATE BALANCE**. Rosemary Harris, George Grizzard, and Elaine Stritch led a stalwart cast who ate and drank that scenery like it was recyclable. It was gripping and thrilling theatre, and yeah, of course it won a bunch of Tonys. This was the Plymouth, after all.

Years would pass before I'd return to the aisles of the Plymouth, this time accepting at last a regular usher spot. I've detailed that in my **JEKYLL & HYDE** story, so let's skip ahead to the show that followed, that chestnut of a musical, **BELLS ARE RINGING**, the classic Judy Holliday vehicle. Now with Faith Prince leading a talented cast including the always reliable Marc Kudisch. With that iconic music and lyrics by Jule Styne, Betty Comden & Adolph Green, **BELLS** would only last a short four months. The *New York Times,* the day after it opened called it a "mothball-soaked revival" in its first paragraph. Yikes.

Ms. Prince would secure a Tony nomination for the role of Bella, but she wouldn't win and in turn, the party was over shortly after that. For her it was said to have been nothing but a dream role for her, but perhaps it came a little too late. I remember that final performance, a hush coming over the audience—and the cast—as Bella sang, with perhaps greater remorse than any other night, one of her big numbers, "The Party's Over." But then she jumped back to life and nailed the final number of "I'm Going Back." A true pro, and again, a score I enjoy listening to. They don't write them like that anymore.

The next show to came in that fall was **THOU SHALT NOT**, which was often referred to by some as **THOU SHOULDN'T HAVE**. With music and lyrics by Harry Connick Jr, directed by Susan Stroman, produced by Lincoln Center, this one had that pedigree all shows wish for—until people saw it. Based on a classic novel by Emile Zola, it was dark and not very tuneful ("Tugboat", anyone?), but it had a great cast: Craig Bierko, Norbert Leo Butz, Kate Levering. A hit on paper, a miss on stage. It opened weeks after 9/11 but by then Broadway audiences weren't in the mood for a story of murder and betrayal set in New Orleans. They wanted something cheery and happy to boost their spirits. **MAMMA MIA** took care of that five blocks north at the Winter Garden.

Jump ahead now to after the runs of **LONG DAY'S JOURNEY** and **TABOO**, both detailed in previous diaries, my final show as a full-time employee at the Plymouth. A play called **MATCH**, starring Frank Langella, Ray Liotta, and Jane Adams (who I knew from "Frasier"). Not the most engaging of plays, and the critics agreed. The show closed after a few months, and I went along with it. I wouldn't return to the Plymouth as a regular, choosing to move on in a new direction.

I've since done three opening nights there as a ticket taker: **THE AUDIENCE**, with Helen Mirren; the unfortunate misfire **CHINA DOLL** starring Al Pacino; and the feel-good 9/11 musical **COME FROM AWAY**. But by that time the theatre had been renamed after Mr. Schoenfeld, an unveiling of its new marquee taking place one afternoon, done in concert with the renaming of the Royale to the Bernard B. Jacobs Theatre, his partner in Broadway's renaissance of the 70s and 80s. Both men had been instrumental in guiding Broadway to its highest standards, and even higher profits.

But to me I sometimes still think of it as the Plymouth, mostly because I'm not done with reliving my history with this famous theatre. And the show I'm talking about—no Tonys.

Still, the show deserves its own chapter, which follows. Think "Plastics."

DIARY FORTY-SIX

# I've Seen Kathleen Turner Naked, and She Has No Idea Who I Am

Ok, I promised one more tale of my ushering life at the Plymouth Theatre, and just to be sure, I won't try and seduce you. Not surprisingly, this was another smash-hit destined to fill the seats of this theatre. Here are the ingredients: take a classic motion picture, adapt it for the stage, cast three A-list stars in the leads, and for shock value, hey, let's drop a towel.

If those aren't enough clues, I'll just say it: **THE GRADUATE**. The 1967 film is iconic—Anne Bancroft, Dustin Hoffman, Katharine Ross. The seduction scene, Benjamin being lured into the world of "plastics," the climactic wedding scene, the bus ride, the music. Memorable moments all, brilliantly directed by Oscar-winner Mike Nichols. So then came the idea to put it on the stage. But did you know it started life as a novel by Charles Webb?

First produced in London, **THE GRADUATE** starred Kathleen Turner in a role tailor-made for her and a-then unknown Matthew Rhys. It ran at the Gielgud Theatre.

I saw it there, but by the time I arrived to the West End a new cast had taken over. The model (and Mick Jagger's girlfriend) Jerry Hall had stepped into the famous role of Mrs. Robinson. I'd bought a good seat for what I thought ended up being a lackluster production—shallow and not well acted.

Maybe the show had lost something during the shift of Hollywood star to stunt-casting.

But the show continued to sell well, so of course it was earmarked for Broadway, with Ms. Turner reprising her role. Joining her on that poster and marquee, and eventually the stage, were Jason Biggs and Alicia Silverstone, of "American Pie" and "Clueless" fame respectively. Talk about buzz surrounding this show. It opened on March 15, 2002. Critics were divided but it didn't matter—we were a huge hit. During the run, JBiggs was fun to hang out with as he'd come to the front of the house before the house opened to chat with the staff. Alicia brought her cute dog every day. Even Ms. Turner even came to the front of the house during a fund-raising for Broadway Cares, but otherwise she stayed backstage.

For nearly a full year, audiences came in droves to see the show, the stars, and yes, the infamous scene where Mrs. Robinson drops her towel. I give huge props to Ms. Turner for braving this role and all the guts—and star-power —it required. This was the third show I'd worked on with her, and even though I'd now seen her naked, she has no idea who I am. (Hence my chapter title!)

A few months into the run, JBiggs had to take a leave of absence to film a Woody Allen movie, so the producers hired an unknown actor to fill in. He wasn't unknown for long. His name? Josh Radnor, and after his turn in **THE GRADUATE** he was cast in the CBS sitcom called "How I Met Your Mother." I tuned into that show initially because of Josh, but I fell in love with all the characters and for nine seasons I had a weekly "Friends" replacement. And of course, that show also reignited NPH's career, our eventual **HEDWIG** Tony winner.

The three original stars would eventually leave after a dedicated run, but not before Ms. Turner's vacation landed up a notable replacement. Linda Gray, of "Dallas" fame, another of my favorite TV shows, played the role for a couple of weeks. There she was, Sue Ellen Ewing, and, um, she too dropped that towel. Look out, JR! But here's a fun fact about Ms. Gray. Do you know she was once a model in her early days and her legs are those in the famous poster for the original movie of **THE GRADUATE**? Full circle.

Then came the replacement cast, and well, things didn't go so well. **THE GRADUATE**'s box office appeal had begun to wane. Lorraine Bracco, fresh off her acclaimed success in "The Sopranos" was our lone headliner. Sorry to say she didn't sell as many tickets, and the two other actors were complete unknowns, and I think remain so.

Not their fault, a thin script needed star-power for it to work; I remember the Friday matinee after Thanksgiving when we had about 250 people in the house. We closed on March 2, 2003, after 380 performances.

But let's go back to that early, infamous scene in the show, when Mrs. Robinson tries to seduce Benjamin. Ms. Turner revealed her full self on a mostly darkened stage, the lightning carefully done to where you could see contours but not…all. A local radio station held a contest for patrons going to see the show, suggesting they scream out "put your clothes on" and one night someone followed through on that "prank." Security promptly tossed the man out and Ms. Turner resumed as if nothing had happened.

She had one more memorable night that I recall. During the scene when the wedding is interrupted toward the end of the show, someone's cell phone rang down front—probably second or third row, house right, directly where Ms. Turner was positioned. She spun around and as only she can do, stared daggers at the person. She held the stare for more than a few Mississippi's. Good for her. Then the show resumed.

Okay, one more story about Ms. Turner. At the opening night of **TABOO**, she came to see the show and our head usher welcomed her back to the Plymouth. She claimed she'd never been in this theatre before (imagine that dark, smoky voice of hers saying that), and when reminded **THE GRADUATE** played here, she said, "No, that was next door." She should have come more often to the front of the house.

But I still adore and respect her craft and dedication to the stage, and I await the time she gets the right role at the right time, so she gets her well-deserved Tony Award. Maybe it'll play the Plymouth. That theatre has a history of Tony wins, even if **THE GRADUATE** came up empty.

DIARY FORTY-SEVEN

# Broadway Dreams and Nightmares

This is a tough one to write. I've been avoiding this entry for, well, apparently forty-six previous diaries, but with my planned number of chapters nearing the end, I guess it's time to talk about the Broadway Theatre. I'll try and be kind. Try is the key word.

As previously detailed, the first Shubert house the office ever sent me to work was at the Broadway—a Thursday night at the original production of **MISS SAIGON**. I was thrilled to work it, see that helicopter descend then lift-off; I knew the score and loved it. I got to see Jonathan Pryce and, in her debut, Lea Salonga.

I would return to work the show a few times over the years, but it was nothing like seeing it the first time. Those soaring melodies, the excitement of the audience, its tragic ending. But I'd come back to the Broadway over the years. I worked Baz Luhrmann's **LA BOHEME** on a Friday night; **BLAST**, which was essentially a concert starring a marching band (don't remember day of week); a Saturday night at **PROMISES, PROMISES** with

Sean Hayes and Kristin Chenoweth, which was lots of fun and had a great score I recalled from childhood; a Sunday matinee at Rodgers and Hammerstein's revived **CINDERELLA**, the final preview of **DOCTOR ZHIVAGO** (I'm in the minority, I liked it—Lucy Simon's score is epic.) I took all those shifts just for a chance to see the shows.

But I did have a short stint there in 2005 when my regular theatre was dark. I was sent there for a week to work at the London-import **BOMBAY DREAMS**, a show, produced by Andrew Lloyd Webber, it was supposed to be a big hit (I had seen it in London and knew it wasn't one), surviving only eight months on Broadway at the so-named Broadway. Ambitious, sure, with some pretty music. But that water fountain set was no helicopter, no chandelier. I would remain with that show for the final three months of the run, the show playing its final performance on New Year's Day.

The next big musical scheduled for the Broadway Theatre was **THE MAMBO KINGS**, based on the book and movie, and I had been told I would be returning. They wanted to keep me! This was the big time, the biggest house in the Shubert chain. Except the show wasn't coming in for eight months, and as things happen on Broadway, it didn't come in at all. Lost its financing, I guess. So off I went to work other theatres.

In 2016, the Broadway Theatre came calling to me again, and in retrospect I wish I'd never answered the phone. Except it was an email, and a directive from the office for a reassignment. **HEDWIG** had closed, I was filling in that fall at the Imperial, but staffing issues were afoot. Two of us ticket takers were being "promoted" from single-person houses to two-person houses. I had asked to remain at the Imperial, since I was comfortable there, but that was not to be because of a corporate rule about family members working together. So that other guy got the Imperial, and I was "offered," as the email stated, the Broadway to work with that man's stepdaughter.

The show playing there was **FIDDLER ON THE ROOF**, which had just opened. I jumped into the job with the gusto I brought to my job as a ticket taker, being the first person to greet the patrons and wish them a good show. The Broadway is the Shubert's largest theatre, at 1,758 seats. But something seemed off from my first day. I felt like a stranger up on 53rd Street. I decided to try and like it there, as I'm never one to run from a tough challenge. **FIDDLER** is an iconic show—I remember playing the score when I took piano lessons as a kid, and my dad loved "If I Were a Rich Man." It was also a treat to work with Danny Burstein again; our paths kept crossing along the Crossroads of the World.

In retrospect, I should have left Anatevka, too, at the time **FIDDLER** closed the following January.

The work atmosphere at the Broadway was always tense, the staff always seemingly on edge each night. But I persevered, rarely took off, and despite being told I wasn't "permanent" there (I was technically in for someone out on disability) according to the management at the theatre, I kept on being invited back show after show. Next up: the revival of **MISS SAIGON**.

I have to say that run of that show remains a blur to me. I'd go in, scan tickets, do my late shifts as needed, enjoy my early shifts when I got to go home. This was also the time when I had made the decision to leave Manhattan behind and move to New Jersey for a life with Steve. I was also working a part-time job during the day, working in a government office in Lower Manhattan, reading and responding to emails for a visually impaired man. I did that job for a year. So, it was a time of flux, when life became all about train schedules and long days. Couldn't I just ask Chris for a ride in that helicopter to get me home faster? Instead, I was left behind like Kim. We would close in January of 2018, not even making it a year. The original production ran for 10 years.

Then came a show, booked for five weeks only, called **ROCKTOPIA**. It mixed classic rock songs with, well, classical music. I worked less than a week there before I moved over to the Jacobs for the longer run (and longer show), of **THE ICEMAN COMETH** with Denzel. The office needed more help at the Jacobs than they did at the Broadway, so I felt we were each doing a favor for the other.

The epic **KING KONG** was next, and I refer readers to Diary #33 for all those details—but it was easily my most favorite time while working as the ticket taker at the Broadway. Kong came into my life, as did my dog, Shadow. I also had a wedding to plan. Take that great experience and juxtapose it with by far my worst experience at the Broadway, the misguided, short-lived revival of **WEST SIDE STORY**. By then my unhappiness working this theatre must have been apparent. It just wasn't a good fit for me, and after five years there (that's some "temporary job!") I was tired of the infighting from some of those who worked there. We should have been focused on our jobs, sure, but still have fun while doing it. Didn't happen. Come on, we're working on Broadway—at the Broadway! Some people just like to promote misery.

This isn't meant to sound bitter. But sometimes not every situation works out.

I would leave the Broadway Theatre abruptly in February of 2020, transferred to the Cort Theatre for the new Tracy Letts play, **THE MINUTES**. Then a few weeks later came the shutdown, and now, as I write this, while Broadway itself is lit up again, the Broadway Theatre remains dark, **WEST SIDE STORY** was one of the few shows not to survive during the pandemic. But I survived, and now thrive again in a new position, with a new company. **THE MINUTES** book a return at Studio 54 in 2022.

The unique and at times unfortunate thing about the Broadway Theatre is that many tourists don't realize it's just the name of the theatre, not every Broadway show is housed through its doors. We would get patrons coming to our doors looking for **PHANTOM, CHICAGO, ALADDIN, THE LION KING**. Not knowing where their shows were playing, they'd just do a Google search for "Broadway theatre" and up came 1681 Broadway on their screen. It happened almost nightly.

Here's my suggestion, and it's only my thought: rename the theatre! If Richard Rodgers has one honoring his contributions to Broadway, might I suggest the Oscar Hammerstein II? That would be one of my favorite things, but I guess it's a message you've got to be carefully taught.

For a while at the Broadway, the heat was on in Saigon. Until it was on me. Mercifully, the nightmare finally closed.

DIARY FORTY-EIGHT

# Are You Ready for Some Football?

Let's get back to some positivity, shall we? I'd like to formally introduce two seemingly disparate world of entertainment pleasures: Hey, Broadway, meet Sports. Hey Sports, meet my world called Broadway. Specifically, it's the game of football, being played not on the field but on a stage.

We're talking **LOMBARDI**, a play by Eric Simonson about legendary Green Bay Packers coach Vince Lombardi. He was so influential in the game of football that the Super Bowl trophy was named after him. What played out on stage, in a 1:45 intermission-free play, was nothing short of transformative. Dan Lauria, the blustery dad from "The Wonder Years," played the blustery Lombardi to absolute perfection. He's good at that, but he also brings a lot of heart and soul to his life lessons. Both to his players, and to the audience.

Then there the luminous, multi-talented Judith Light, Tony-nominated for her performance as Marie Lombardi, who offered up her own brand of wisdom, along with a drink or two. I'll just plain say it: I adore Ms. Light beyond words. We have a bit of history, and she remains one of my favorite actresses—TV or on stage, and one on my most favorite people to greet at theatre. She is a huge supporter of our industry.

I was first "introduced" to her as Karen Wolek on the ABC soap opera "One Life to Live" (TV guilty pleasure #1 for me, bar none), and then she of course went on to star in ABC's "Who's the Boss" with Tony Danza. But this actress has such depth and a warmth to her, a way to engage the audience with whatever the script calls for. She was so calculating on the reboot of Dallas on TNT and was amazing in **WIT** during its off-Broadway run. She also won two consecutive Tony Awards for **OTHER DESERT CITIES** at the Booth and **THE ASSEMBLED PARTIES** at the Friedman.

I first met Ms. Light at, believe it or not—this is one of my favorite life moments ever — the 1996 Democratic National Convention in Chicago. As I had edited a book (that's my publishing career) called "Capitol Offense," written by Maryland Senator Barbara Mikulski and her political insider friend, Marylouise Oates, I was invited to introduce them at their morning "coffee klatch" book signing. There's me, Joe on the big stage—I barely slept the night before while preparing my speech. But aside from being awed by witnessing Senator Ted Kennedy buying two copies of the book at the event, I got to say hello to Ms. Light and her husband, actor Robert

Desiderio. She had bought the television rights to the book and was planning to make it into a made-for-TV movie, with the idea of it going to series. Alas, it never got filmed.

Cut to **LOMBARDI**. It's the Tuesday after the Tony nominations were announced, and I'm sitting in the lower lobby of Circle in the Square. Mr. Lauria was being interviewed by someone from the press, and then arrives Ms. Light for that night's performance. I nodded hello as she started to head backstage, but not before she paused, looked back, and said, "Why do I know you?" I reminded her of the story of our meeting, and she said, "I told my husband about this usher and that I knew you from politics."

She is a lovely woman and a consummate professional, embodying whatever character she is portraying with depth and feeling. When we see each other at the theatre I now get a Judith hug at the door. She's so special and has earned all of her accolades and awards.

As for **LOMBARDI** itself, I enjoyed the show. Football is not my favorite sport (baseball is), but I appreciated the backstory of the trophy and the man it became named after. The script, based on a best-selling book, went beyond the gridiron and into the human emotions behind those who are so passionate about the sport. We would have theme nights at Circle—there were times a Super Bowl trophy was on display in a glass case, a way to get sports fans to Broadway. It worked for a while.

Also helpful for ticket sales was the fact that the Green Bay Packers won the Super Bowl the year **LOMBARDI** played Circle. That drove the crowds to us, but unfortunately it would wane. Despite a Friday night when the entire New York Jets team showed up to see the show, despite one of the producers being the influential Mara family, who owned the Giants and loved showing off their trophy in that glass case, **LOMBARDI'S** season was coming to a close. No playoffs here, the show ended before the Tony ceremony in June, on May 22, 2011. 244 performances.

But for five months on those aisles, I enjoyed my return to Circle in the Square. It's such a unique space and at times I would be asked to direct the audience to their aisles at the base of the escalator. One night my dentist showed up! So out of context. And sometimes I would be asked to be ticket taker. We also had a "floater usher" position; that employee worked the lobby and assisted patrons who needed to use the accessible restroom, unable to take the stairs. I did that job often, and it required me to take patrons down an elevator and along a corridor inside the Paramount building. Circle kept our jobs interesting.

The creators and producers of **LOMBARDI** would try for a hat trick of Broadway and Sports—**MAGIC/BIRD** premiered at the Longacre, and sad to say it didn't last long, and **BRONX BOMBERS**, which would take up residence at Circle. That didn't work either. Not all games play well on the stage, or the field. Or perhaps it was the blend of the message **LOMBARDI** imparted to his players, as well as the ensemble team of actors who understood that the story they were telling went beyond the stadium, and into the theatre, and in fact, real life.

## DIARY FORTY-NINE

# Jesus Takes the Circle

This is how I began the original Facebook entry of this one: "Hi Everyone, it's Joseph the Worker." I decided to not edit that out for this entry. See, that's who I was told I was named after. You know, the stalwart guy back in biblical times who just happened to play a role in helping Mary give birth to a rather famous figure in history. It's kind of ironic that in my entire life I've held multiple jobs at the same time. Daytime, nighttime, weekends. I am living up to the "worker" bee in me.

But this isn't about me, not really, it's about **GODSPELL**, the well-known, often-produced, sometimes maligned show about Jesus and his followers. But in this entry, I'm going to attempt to build a beautiful city, with all God's gifts, day by day, brick by brick. I just love this show and its message.

My first exposure to the music of **GODSPELL** was in high school chorale. We sang "Day by Day," probably the show's best-known song. I got to sing the beautiful melody of "Beautiful City," probably my favorite song from the show. What did I do as an eager theatre-lover (geek?) back then at the age of 15? I bought the Original Cast Recording. I stared at that iconic artwork, I read the liner notes, poured over the track listings...and I found no sign of a song called "Beautiful City." Turns out, it wasn't in the original production, only added to the feature film version.

**GODSPELL** began as a college project, then played off-off-Broadway before transferring to a hit run off-Broadway in 1971 at the Cherry Lane Theatre, then later moved to the Promenade Theatre n the Upper West Side. Probably its biggest success was the Toronto production in 1972, which launched the careers of actors like Victor Garber, Eugene Levy, Andrea Martin, Gilda Radner, Dave Thomas, Martin Short, and its musical director, Paul Shaffer. The show would later transfer to Broadway at the Broadhurst in 1976.

Most of that cast attended the opening night of **GODSPELL**'s Broadway revival at Circle in the Square on November 7, 2011. I was there—hell, they were all on my aisle! Among the actors in the show were some known celebs, like Hunter Parish in the role of Jesus, fresh off his success in TV's "Weeds," and some upcoming stage stars like the beautiful voices of Telly Leung, Lindsey Mendez, Nick Blaemire, and Uzo Abudu. Corbin Bleu would take over for Hunter eventually.

Now, let's get on to the memories from the show. The Belasco was once again dark (again) after the production of **WOMEN ON THE VERGE** shut down in January 2011, so I ended up back at my second favorite theatre, Circle in the Square. I loved working with all those ladies — Georgia, Sofie, Margie, and the rest of the Circle gang, Cheryl and Kelly and Jayson and Allyson. We had a lot of fun back then.

What's great about Circle is that the actors enter through the front doors, same as us. They would walk through the lower lobby toward backstage, but that meant they would stop, say hi, we'd say hi back, and not unlike the spirit of that was **GODSPELL** a communal spirit, a unity, was established. There was no separation of "us" and "them," so unlike many other shows I had worked over the years at other theatres. Circle is aptly named. We may be a bit square too.

**GODSPELL** was a relatively easy enough show to work. Circle only had about 750 seats for this staging, and it used all four sections for this production, so it truly was theater in the round. The actors would make their entrances down the stairs at the top of aisles 1 or 3, or through what's called the "vom," full name the vomitorium, a reference to the escape routes gladiators used when trying to evade the lions attacking them in Rome's Colosseum.

Imagine that image when, at intermission, I was sent down to "work" the vom. On the west side of the house, I'd get to chat with Wallace Smith, who played Brutus (and who I'd later work with at **ROCKY**). Other nights I'd be on the east side of the house, where Hunter made his Act II entrance. I'd nod his way and say, "Good Evening, Jesus." He had a bright, toothy smile, which he'd produce when I'd say those words. But my primary job at those voms was to ensure patrons didn't think that exit would get them to the bathrooms!

A few thoughts about the performances. Telly sang the hell out of "All God's Gifts," and Lindsey Mendez brought down the house with "Bless the Lord." But the high point was Uzo's Act II song, "By My Side." Haunting and beautiful, I thought to myself, "Who is this woman?" Well, she's been in high demand ever since making her Broadway debut, winning Emmy's for "Orange is the New Black," among other credits.

Then there was Hunter's "Beautiful City." Flash back to high school, my own voice singing those words, knowing them almost by heart even then watching this show all these years later. His voice was soft, perhaps reedy, but the emotion behind those words quieted the house and cast a solemn glow all around Circle. It was the emotional highlight for me and also the beginning of his character's resurrection. Life's affirmation in duality.

I would think of my dad. The Deacon. Circle, like the Belasco, brings him to life.

**GODSPELL** would close on June 24, 2012, a respectable run of eight months but it was not a profitable one. Also, it would not receive any Tony nominations, which was a shame. Lindsey has since won a Tony for her role as Carrie in **CAROUSEL** And speaking of her, and Telly for that matter, I'd like to give them a shout out here. During the run of **GODSPELL**, we had these "pillow" seats down on the floor, situated just before the edge of the stage. The cast would invite one audience member to help act out a scene involving "Lazarus," which included speaking lines on the stage; Telly and Lindsey would direct that person on what to say, when to say them. Here was my plan. I arranged, with their help, to get my niece, the Broadway-wannabe with the powerful belting voice, Jennifer, chosen.

Trouble was, she was with a few college friends, and they kept changing pillow locations within their designated seating area. The person who was picked to go up on stage had to be seated on a certain pillow—and Jen kept moving! I finally had to go down the aisle and point toward the pillow she should remain on. I said, "Don't move." See, she had no idea of the surprise I'd planned.

She got to make her Broadway debut!

Ok, Joseph the Worker's work here is done.

DIARY FIFTY

# Another Opening, Another Closing

Much like I did with an earlier entry about Circle in the Square and the "quick hits" of shows I'd worked there, in this entry I'm giving the Belasco the same treatment. I've worked so many shows at that theatre, most of them unintentionally short runs or limited runs because… well, prior to the renovation (and sometimes after), producers weren't fans of its east of Broadway location. Foot traffic means a lot in Times Square.

Here are some highlights (and maybe some lowlights) of some of the shows I saw and/or worked:

**SACRILEGE** staring Ellen Burstyn, which closed quickly. **ENCHANTED APRIL** where I got see Molly Ringwald live in stage! Wasn't a pretty run. I actually just sat in a seat, working neither of those shows. Then there were the shows I did work, most of which would close within a few months of opening night. The Belasco had an odd history of opening a show in April and then closing on the day of the Tony Awards in June. **JOURNEY'S END** did this, as did **HONOUR** with Jane Alexander,

Laura Linney and Robert Foxworth (of "Falcon Crest"). Tony day usually coincided with the Puerto Rican day parade, and as it happened 44$^{th}$ Street and 6$^{th}$ Avenue was used as a staging area for the parade's floats. Our plays would have to compete against the pulsing music playing on the street outside.

I would work a few shows at the Belasco once, feeling like a guest star in my own house. Usually, a Monday night when my regular house was dark, I'd pick up that extra shift. I got to see **FOLLIES**, the Roundabout production starring Blythe Danner, Treat Williams and others. A show about an old theatre and the ghosts that live within it, the Belasco was an ideal home for this. It was almost like the house was part of the set. I'd work **DRACULA**, too, with Tom Hewitt and Melissa Errico. I liked it, mostly because I do like Frank Wildhorn's pop/Broadway music and the cast was uber-talented. But the staging had some questionable choices. I'll leave it at that.

Then one Sunday night I worked **JAMES JOYCE'S THE DEAD**; a chamber musical based on his short story. Christopher Walken headlined the show, but I recognized another name in the cast. An actor named Brian Davies, and before I could say "Holy Victoria Lord Buchanan," who comes to my aisle but none other than the grand dame of "One Life to Live" Erika Slezak—Mr. Davies' wife! I'd met them once before (we had lunch together, a publishing career story!) and she remembered me, and said, "Oh yes, you mentioned you also worked on Broadway." She's won six Leading Actress Emmys. Just….um, wow. What a classy woman. Her father was the famous actor Walter Slezak, who starred in Alfred Hitchcock's "Lifeboat." My favorite director and one of my favorite actresses, conjoined by history.

Sometimes I love my job.

Tony-winner Mandy Patinkin came to the Belasco Theatre for a run of his one-man show, **MAMALOSHEN**. They were all songs sung in Yiddish, just Mandy and his piano accompanist on that stage. What did the staff like about this show? Only six performances a week (we got paid for eight), and the running time was just over an hour with no intermission. Except that would change as the run progressed. Perhaps realizing his fans were coming to hear more, he started adding songs people expected to hear. Think Sondheim.

Also, Mandy's wife, Kathryn Grody, performed her one-woman show, **A MOM'S LIFE**, at the Belasco every Monday during the run. Nice work if you can get it!

Speaking of nice work, and I did get it, now I get to write about the unexpected, odd, quirky, surprisingly classy (at times) and crude, funny, and silliest show I think I've ever ushered in all these years. In a word: **JACKIE**. Written by Gil Hoppe and originally produced at Harvard's Hasty Pudding troop, this was one wacky play, but also one that had a bit of grace. I'll explain.

Okay, so this was a play about the life of one-time first lady Jacqueline Bouvier Kennedy Onassis. From her upbringing, her marriage to JFK, her life after when she married Greek tycoon Aristotle Onassis, it was a piece of history, but done in a mix of styles that I think ultimately left the (small) audience confused as to what they were watching. What was the point of view?

Ten actors played various roles, all of them incredibly talented and able to switch out of character and into another at a moment's notice. I remember Victor Slezak as JFK and a sweaty Derek Smith as Nixon during that infamous debate; Thomas Derrah played a crazy Onassis, always pulling up his sagging pants with exaggerated mannerisms and speaking loudly for comic effect.

Then there were the puppets. We're not talking **AVENUE Q** style, these were larger than life, big-headed and with thunderous voices—especially patriarch Joseph Kennedy. When he made his entrance while his sons—JFK, Bobby, Teddy —were playing football on the grounds of their estate, a voice from somewhere bellowed, "Where is the new girl?"

Ah, that's brings us to the new girl. That's where we come to the graceful part of my tale. TV actress and co-star of the film "Independence Day" Margaret Colin played the role of Jackie, and what she accomplished was grounding the silliness going on around her. I remember her sitting in an apartment studio set on stage, staring into a telescope, as though she was taking a lens to her own life. She spoke reverently, gently, and darn if she didn't look the part.

**JACKIE: A NEW COMEDY** was a massive flop that ran for six months. We'd have houses of 150 people some nights, barely filling the front rows of the orchestra. The balcony was nearly always closed. We just moved down people who'd bought those cheaper seats to the mezzanine. Thank you American Express for underwriting this show. It kept our staff working, despite the office once referring to that show as "charity." Yeah, it kinda was. But hey, we were sold out on Valentine's Day, even the balcony, where I was taking tickets at the side door.

Three more shows left to talk about, if you can bear it. One a big misfire, the other a limited run, and the other: pure crazy.

Let's do the misfire first. David Mamet's **AMERICAN BUFFALO** came in starring John Leguizamo, Cedric the Entertainer, and Haley Joel Osment ("I see dead people"—more like, in this case, "I see dead shows"). We started previews in October 2008, the show playing concurrently with the more appealing **SPEED THE PLOW**. It seemed to be a Mamet-fest that season, but there were complications on our end. See, Mamet wasn't involved in this production. Acclaimed director Robert Falls helmed this show, but I could sense from that first preview…something was off. The audience came to see our stars and were expecting to laugh at this drama. And laugh they did.

Reviews were scathing. We opened on a Monday night and closed that following Sunday. One week of performances, just before the Thanksgiving week (which usually meant higher ticket sales.) I guess the producers knew when to cut their losses. I recall an elderly patron speaking to his wife as they exited the Belasco one night: "Well, it's going to be a while before we see this show back on Broadway." (A revival is set to open at Circle in the Square in 2022, with Laurence Fishborne, Sam Rockwell, and Darren Criss.)

In 2012, **GOLDEN BOY** by Clifford Odets was another revival from the folks at Lincoln Center Theater and director Bartlett Sher, with a terrific ensemble, starring such actors like Tony Shaloub, Yvonne Strahovski, Seth Numrich, and once again appearing on that Belasco stage, the versatile Danny Burstein. It was a limited run and received great reviews, if only the complicated set would stop breaking down! Fun fact here, the original production of **GOLDEN BOY** played the same theatre in 1937.

Okay, now let's have some fun and see if comedienne Kathy Griffin can win herself a Tony. At least, that's how the show was billed up on the marquee: officially, **KATHY GRIFFIN WANTS A TONY**. A two-week run in March of 2011, 10 shows only, it was a chance for her to play Broadway and just cut loose with an obviously adoring fan base. So much so that one patron tried to grab a full stack of *Playbills* off an aisle—before he'd been seated. I said he couldn't have that many. "Oh, who's the power bitch now!"

That was an indication of the crowd we were going to get for that show.

But I had specific duties given to me for **GRIFFIN**. See, for most performances she'd bring out a special guest at the top of the show; they'd help get the audience revved up for all the gossipy nonsense and frivolity to follow. The celebrity would remain on stage for only a couple of minutes of banter and then they would make their exit off stage to be seated. How did they find those seats? With my help. One of the producers of the show had been watching me in action during the walk-in, directing people to their seats, and so I was chosen to help escort the celebs to their seats after their on-stage entrance.

Think: Rosie O'Donnell, Rachael Ray, and appropriately, Tony Roberts. Kathy at least got one Tony. That was the (haha) joke that night. But it was fun to meet them each at what's called the "pass-door" on house right and escort them to their seat. I'd already been given advance word of their aisle and row. It was always an aisle seat. I never met Ms. Griffin.

Later that season we were supposed to get the Broadway debut of Neil LaBute's **FAT PIG**. Never came in, again, a case of a show losing its financing.

Oh, the Belasco. A tortured history, a few big hits, memorable flops, but in the end, fueling one of the best memories of my theatrical life. In fact, I've got one more Belasco story to tell…it's a great way to wrap up these diaries. To paraphrase Shakespeare, "Wherefore art thou, David?"

DIARY FIFTY-ONE

# Mulled Wine for Everyone

Dim the electricity, light the many sundry candles and get ready to immerse yourself in a bygone era. Shakespeare, the way his plays were intended to be performed—no offense to modern takes on his plays that expose new truths to his words and our world. But right now, we are going old-school. Back at the Belasco—yeah, once again, and perhaps the most perfect house to transport its audience back to simpler times, with the Globe's productions of **TWELFE NIGHT** and **RICHARD III**.

Tony-award winner Mark Rylance brought his merry troupe of thespians from across the "pond," setting up residence at the Belasco Theatre for a six-month run of two Shakespeare plays, one a comedy, which would be performed six times a week, and then a history play, done twice a week. Both proved equally popular, as we were sold out every single performance.

Previews began on October 15, 2013, with an official opening on November 10. Truth be told, I wasn't sure I was going to be part of the staff there. See, I'd taken the ticket taker job at the Lyceum, first for **THE NANCE**, then A **NIGHT WITH JANIS JOPLIN**. I liked being a TT, so I was prepared to remain in my current position until…until, the Belasco's long-term ticket taker, Kitty, decided to move away from the city, thus not returning to her job.

Cue the Belasco's manager phone call to me, informing me that if I wanted the job to notify the office and request the position. The Shubert office kind of expected my email. Long and short, I was returned to the Belasco, again, this time as the full-time ticket taker, and I'll tell you, I loved being back "home," but it was an intense experience working a big hit there. Not how the Belasco normally rolled. **TWELFE NIGHT/RICHARD III** was a unique experience in many respects.

First, there was the ticket demand from customers. The box office was super busy, like I'd never witnessed at the Belasco. And this was even before the rave reviews. We didn't permit patrons to wait in our small lobby before the walk-in, it would just get too crowded, so they had to form a line out in front of the theatre. I would help organize eager theatergoers, which included making a separate line for those patrons who had tickets for our special stage seating. Yup, there were about 50 seats on both sides of the stage, giving the audience an up-close of the actors and their Shakespearean proceedings.

When the manager announced the house was open, we would bring in the stage-seats patrons first, let them use the facilities or whatever they needed, because we wanted them in their seats as quickly as possible. Late seating for stage seats wasn't viable once the show began. And then the rest of the audience would pour in, and even though the Belasco was a single ticket taker house (me...), there were times when the head usher opened another door to help with a sudden rush. We had nearly 1,080 seats for this production and 30 minutes to get every patron in.

What was awesome about the producers, including lead producer Sonia Friedman (whom I'd worked with at Circle for **THE NORMAN CONQUESTS**) decided all balcony seats were $25, thus making Broadway more accessible to many more people, young people, students. Yeah, that balcony may be high, but not since **THE CRUCIBLE** had I seen those seats put to better use for these impressive, and impressionable, shows.

I'd never been a huge Shakespeare fan. I did take a course in college as part of my English studies where we read his plays, but I found the text challenging to absorb. I still prefer my prose more mystery/spy thriller, and none of them are written in iambic pentameter. But there was such care given to this material, to the words, the language, and the actors, from Rylance, Stephen Fry, and so many others, there was love and respect being delivered on the Belasco stage. The audience could feel the love. Word of mouth kept us sold-out.

Okay, enough respect, let's get to the behind-the-scenes stuff. In the spacious basement of the Belasco, our British visitors set up a home away from home. A pool table, TVs, sofas, a bar, it's where the cast would spend their off time, giving them a sense of the familiar (read: English pub). There would be occasional parties after the show, which all staff were invited to. We even rallied everyone to do a Secret Santa and had a crazy night of exchanging gifts with our fellow Shakespeareans. Among my gifts was a coffee mug printed with a quote from John Waters: "If you go home with someone and they don't have books, don't (expletive) them." My Santa knew I was a writer and reader.

Another fun experience happened in the lobby preshow on a Saturday matinee. I was busy setting up my scanners when I noticed a rather famous actress looking befuddled—as only she can do. It was none other than Teri Hatcher, one of my TV favorites (I loved her in "Lois and Clark" and liked "Desperate Housewives," but most memorably, on "Seinfeld."). She'd inadvertently purchased three tickets to **TWELFE NIGHT**, but only needed two. I brought her to the box office; they easily bought the extra ticket back knowing they could resell it. She was so excited (she even got cash for the ticket return), that she hugged me. She said, "Hi, I'm Teri." I then congratulated her on winning her recent celebrity edition of Food Network's "Chopped." She was spectacular. (Reference, anyone?)

The producers also gave the audience a special treat on what was the actual "twelfe night," during the holiday season. Downstairs in the lounge were cases of mulled wine, which the bar staff had been instructed to hand out free small glasses of the wine during the walk-in to each patron of age. I got to inform the crowd lined-up outside to make sure they stopped at the bar to take part in the British tradition. (I even got to take home a leftover bottle.)

I know this is going on long, but I've got one more tale to tell. Who was a big fan of these shows and came several times to see them, bringing family and friends each time, including on our dual-opening night? Joan Rivers. She was so sweet and filled with *joie de vivre*. I always enjoyed welcoming her back to the Belasco. At the party later that evening at Gotham, I got to speak with her and grabbed one of my most favorite pictures ever, she and I glammed up for the special night.

Mark Rylance would be nominated for Best Actor for **RICHARD III** and Best Featured Actor for **TWELFE NIGHT**. He'd win for the latter. The shows themselves racked up six Tony nominations and served as a reminder that iambic pentameter is alive and well in this modern age. And, I also got to become friends with a frequent patron, a sweet lady in a pink scarf.

The Belasco never glowed like it did during our British invasion, yes because of the candles that lit the stage but because of the natural energy given off by cast, crew, audience. A final thanks to the famed Stephen Fry for his closing party (he left the show four-days before the actual closing) at the Lion's Club on West 44th Street. The manager and I presented him with a framed photograph of the Belasco's marquee. Lastly, the PR firm produced a calendar to memorialize the productions, each month including photos of cast, crew, and for the month of December—yeah, the front of house staff, captioning the photo with the phrase "the best house staff on Broadway." Thanks to them for including us in the history of this production. Though years have passed, I still have that calendar, as though, like Shakespeare, it can always be looked at with a fresh eye and a sense of history.

Oh, wait, one last story. A coda to an earlier story. One Saturday matinee, Tyne Daly came to see **TWELFE NIGHT** and after the show ended, I was locking up the lobby access door, ready for my dinner break. Who returns? Ms. Daly. She'd forgotten her *Playbill* and was hoping to get a fresh one. I went back in the house to fetch her one, and upon my return I was torn whether what I wanted to say to her should be said. But I told her.

"One of the first shows I worked on Broadway was your **GYPSY** at the St. James."

She paused, assessed me, and said, "What, were you 10?"

I was 25 years old when I worked that show. Some People are so nice.

DIARY FIFTY-TWO

# The 11 O'clock Number

Closings of shows were always filled with mixed emotions. Sometimes a long run would sing or say its earned goodbye, or a limited run would ride off amidst its critical glory. Or a show with good intentions just didn't get the support from crowds and critics and had to put up that dreaded notice backstage.

For me, well, I'm going to put up my notice, too, as this chapter is our closing night. After a year spent writing these recollections, it's time to condense 30 years of Broadway life and history into some final thoughts. It's time for my 11:00 O'clock number.

There's an old story about the derivation of that phrase, the 11:00 O'clock number. Aren't we all headed home by that time, the show is over, the bows taken, and the curtain having come down, the exit music playing its final note? A lone stagehand has already placed the ghost light on the stage until the next performance, or in the case of a closing, the next show. It's a quiet time in the theatre, me downstairs, usually changing into my street clothes and then leaving a darkened house.

It would often be 12:00 midnight by the time I got home.

But back in Broadway's early days, curtain time was at 8:30, so by the time the show (they were longer back then, no 90-minute intermission-less shows back then) reached the eleventh hour, it was time for the big number! I always think of "Rose's Turn" from **GYPSY** as the ultimate, but of course there are many other examples that I'm sure fans have.

Just think of all those shows you've seen and that impactful moment during the last act when you found yourself on the edge of your seat. Knowing greatness was about to burst forth on that stage and send you home with one last bit of razzle dazzle.

In this modern era of Broadway, curtain times are varied, depending on the show and the night. Weeknights gravitate toward earlier curtains, at 7:00 pm. Friday and Saturday nights remain mostly traditional, 8:00 pm start times (with a Saturday matinee at 2:00). Sunday is a mixed bag—usually 3:00 pm, unless your show has a 2:00, and then there's another at night, at 7:00 or 7:30. For those of us who work on the Great White Way, we've got to be on our toes and be aware of the ever-changing and varied start times.

But the notion, concept, the very idea, of the 11:00 number remains in spirit and tradition. It's supposed to leave the audience touched, exhilarated, the number usually an encapsulation of all that you've just experienced for the last couple of hours. It's also usually not the final number of the show. I like to think of "What I Did for Love," from **A CHORUS LINE** as the 11:00 number, but then the audience is treated to the singular sensation that is "One."

My 11:00 o'clock number would be called 41. The exact number of Broadway theatres that surround this world we call Broadway, and I'd like to imagine how that song would have sounded over the many decades. Which composer could have written such an encompassing song? A witty tune from Rodgers and Hart, a brilliantly orchestrated piece by Leonard Bernstein, the twinkling piano of Gershwin? How about a tuneful Rodgers and Hammerstein's melody but with powerful lyrics, Sondheim's crafty words and complex music playing with the concept of 41, Andrew Lloyd Webber's memorable bombast in a soaring anthem? My mind veers toward classic interpretations, too, by Porter, Berlin, Styne. Kander & Ebb giving the song some needed class. I'd actually like my 11 O'clock song to be written by Cy Coleman, because he always knew how to compose and capture the perfect mood of the theme of one of his shows. Did **BARNUM** sound like a circus?

I write this piece as I am working at the Gershwin Theatre, surrounded by photographs of all the people who have been inducted into the Theatre Hall of Fame. Belasco's photograph is one pillar away from my workstation. I always think of Broadway as being alive with ghosts, an ironic twist of words. Faces stare back at me here, and I imagine their nights, their very lives, spent on the stage, devoted to a craft, now forever recognized with awards and accolades, and deservedly so.

But there are so many other members of this place we call Broadway. Imagine the number of people it takes to put on a show, whether play or musical, it would surprise many a theatergoer. How many stagehands, electricians, or players in the orchestra, and what about stage management, wardrobe, the press office, producers, security, the ticket sellers both online and in the box office, and of course, because it was my department, front of the house.

As evidenced through my theatrical memoir, I've worked a LOT of theatres. Broadway is a bit of a transient business, you go where the work takes you. Sometimes you land a long-running show and you remain at that show and theatre, or sometimes, a frequent question pops up among us ushers: "Is you're your house?" Sometimes, yeah, you work the same show for 30-plus years (**THE PHANTOM OF THE OPERA,** anyone?). But sometimes you land at a house with its own unique history of short runs, flops, and occasional hits. Then you move on, for the work and for the love of theatre, thankful to always be welcomed back through those stage doors.

Yes, 41 Theatres at current count. I've worked 33 of them as of March 12, 2020.

In these pages, I've detailed my life at all 17 of the Shubert-owned theatres: so many stories from my beloved

Belasco, but also the Lyceum, Cort, Shubert, Broadhurst, Majestic, Golden, Royale/Jacobs, Plymouth/Schoenfeld, Booth, Imperial, Music Box, Barrymore, Ambassador, Longacre, Winter Garden, and way up on 53rd Street, the Broadway.

But I give acknowledgment also to the nine Nederlander houses which influenced my early days: Nederlander, Marquis, Palace, Minskoff, Richard Rodgers, Brooks Atkinson, Neil Simon, Gershwin, and lastly, finally, the Lunt-Fontanne, which I finally worked in my new job.

Jujamcyn, I've only worked three of their five theatres as an usher, four if you include my new job renting out headsets to those who need hearing assistance: I'm talking the Eugene O'Neill, Virginia/August Wilson, St. James, Martin Beck/Hirschfeld and the elusive Walter Kerr.

As for the independents and non-profits, I've never worked the American Airlines, Henry Miller/Sondheim, Helen Hayes, Studio 54, Biltmore/Friedman, New Amsterdam, Hudson, though I did work, at last, the Lyric. Farthest uptown is the Vivian Beaumont, Lincoln Center Theater's Broadway house. I've worked there but only a handful of times. And of course, last but not least, the wonderful Circle in the Square.

Each of these theatres house a treasure of people, plays, musicals and special events, some surviving for over a century, while others with only decades beneath their wings. So many other theatres were built back during Broadway's golden age, but time can be cruel to artistry and to architecture, progress always the enemy of the arts. We lost the Morosco, the original Helen Hayes, the Bijou. But in turn we got the Marquis, which is where I got my start—so I can't be too upset.

But if I've learned anything in writing this book, it's that memories don't fade away, they somehow become enhanced, often triggered by a song, a new show, the passing of a treasured co-worker or actors. That ghost light I've spoken of holds all these buildings in its glow, never to be silenced or dimmed.

When I started to work on Broadway, I told myself I'd come for the shows, and yes, if I'm being honest, for the paycheck too, but in the final analysis I stayed for the theatres. Walking those aisles, exploring their nooks and crevices and learning their storied secrets, meeting great people along the way. Ultimately, though, and here's the lesson I learned: I remained for the history, and maybe in some way, I hope, I like to think, that I've made a small contribution.

Broadway is a community that might only stretch from 41$^{st}$ to 65$^{th}$ Street, but in a way, it's bigger than that. Broadway is not just a street, it's a concept, a collective state of mind, where what happens on those stages remains there, except after the curtain falls, where it's relegated to a mind richly filled with magical memories.

May the curtain forever rise again. In fact, Everybody, Rise!

ENCORE

# The Bishop of Broadway Strikes Again

One final truth that I've learned, and it's one you only need to learn once: don't mess with ghosts.

There are moments when I'm home and its late night, or perhaps early morning is more apt, like a recent night at 4:00 a.m. when I felt a chill rip through me. Not just cold, an inner sense of another presence swirling around me. It can be unsettling. Even Shadow at 6:00 a.m. started to wail, something stirring him from his usual deep sleep.

That makes me think of the Lion in "The Wizard of Oz," as he says, "I do believe in spooks, I do believe in spooks," while he tugs at his tail. I'm with you. Grabbing for some courage. But what that chilly sense settling within me truly dug up was a memorable moment at the Belasco. A bit of backstory before I get to the real story of that Friday night in 2015.

As legend tells it, the ghost of David Belasco continues to be ever-present at his namesake theatre on West

44th Street. Several ushers and stagehands have told stories of having seen the "Bishop of Broadway," known for his black suits and white, priest-like collar. He supposedly was disgusted by the production of "Oh, Calcutta" in the 70s, and on opening night he thrust open the rear doors and made his exit.

But he returned home at some point and remains to this day…and beyond. There is a 10-room apartment above the theatre where Belasco lived and worked. He wrote and produced many shows at his theatre, and obviously had a love for the building he'd had built. I don't disagree with him. It's well documented in this book that it's my favorite Broadway house to work, or to visit.

When I took on the position of ticket taker during the run of **TWELFE NIGHT/RICHARD III**, and next, for the run of **HEDWIG AND THE ANGRY INCH**, I'd be scanning tickets at the main door while a portrait of Belasco stared back at me from the left wall of the lobby. I once took a picture of it and I swear there was a ghostly glow in the background of the photo. Perhaps just residue from a flash—or perhaps something more otherworldly. I like to think he liked me. Hmm, maybe not.

Back in the 1990s, the manager's office at the Belasco, located above the box office in the lobby, housed David's big wooden desk, a great piece of furniture crafted from a bygone era. When the then-manager was switched up to the Cort, he took the desk with him. I don't imagine that sat well with its original owner.

Years later, during **HEDWIG**, the desk would finally be returned to its rightful place in the manager's office at the Belasco, much to the pleasure of the current manager. This moment would coincide with what would have been Belasco's 162$^{nd}$ birthday, and we intended to have a birthday party for him—and to celebrate the desk's return home. We had cake, and all the ushers and staff were set to gather upstairs in the manager's office before walk-in that night.

I was late to the party, as I was in the lobby setting up my four scanners in preparation of that night's sold-out performance. An idea came to me on how to make a fashionably late entrance. Dressed in my black suit, black shirt and tie—-looking very Regis Philbin circa "Who Wants to Be a Millionaire," I grabbed one of the bar napkins and folded it under my collar, thus giving me a priestly look. Not only was the desk back, but so too was The Bishop.

Thinking this idea would be fun, the box office buzzed me through the door that led to the upstairs office. Everyone was already gathered there. I started to flick the light switch at the bottom of the steps, on and off, on and off, slowly creeping up the stairs and announcing to all, "This is the ghost of David Belasco," using a creepy voice as taken from an old horror movie.

I actually scared a few of the ushers, but the prank was mostly well-received. Well, not by everyone. Because then came Belasco's revenge.

Cake eaten, desk cleared and the house ready to open, I went to my scanners I'd just set up and they suddenly weren't working. But fifteen minutes previously they were all working fine. I checked the battery strength and found they were drained to nothing. Despite an attempt at a reboot, there was no way I could get them charged in five minutes before we started taking tickets. So that night I had to tear over 1,000 tickets the old-fashioned way, making sure I got all the bar codes to be later scanned into the system when I got those scanners up and running. It was a hectic walk-in.

**HEDWIG** began, and then I did my usual job of returning the scanners to their chargers in the manager's office, and that's when I noticed the power-strip we used for the four scanners' chargers had been pulled from the wall outlet. Now, I'm not saying what exactly happened, perhaps it got knocked out accidentally by a stagehand or moving guy when the old desk was restored inside the office, or maybe, just maybe, someone didn't like my impression and decided to remind me whose name lit up that marquee outside.

There are occasional tours of "ghostly New York," and this one docent would always bring her customers to the Belasco Theatre among her stops. I got to be familiar with her as she led her small but curious group of customers. I once told her this story, and from that point forward she would make a point to stop by and ask me to recount this tale for the ghostly curious. I would always tell the folks, "In the end, I had to defer to the Bishop and extend my apology to him. After all, it's his theatre." But I like to think that for 30 years, on and off, I was a pretty good caretaker of the Belasco's history, always looking toward its future, remembering him and his contribution to the continuing lore that is Broadway.

And I suppose, me playing a keeper of the ghosts that swirl around all these theatres, keeping alive their stories, their pasts and hoping to ensure future shows, future audiences, future staff members who will be forever changed by such an experience. Yes, shows come and go, new openings keep the lights burning and the marquee lit. But those ghosts never leave, they don't ever post a closing notice.

What an honor to have been, and continue to be, part of this life we call, simply, by one word, but one that means so much: Broadway.

## ACKNOWLEDGMENTS:

So many people to thank.

House Managers: Stephanie, Joe, Thia, Shawn, Michelle, Carolyne, Joann, Cheryl

Head Ushers: Dexter, Georgia, Francine, Raya, Debbie, Helen, John, Dennis, William

Box Office: Al, Gary, Brian, Bill, Michael, Rachel, Jose, Tommy, Laura, Steven, Jen, Melissa, Shari, Rianna

More Front of House: Caroline, Rosa, Monica, Yolanda, Carmen, Terri, Carrie, Marco

Security: Annie, Jerry, Joey, Mike, Doc, Joon, Fred, Jim, another Mike, so many others

All of Shubert security: Amos and the gang.

Too many ushers to name: you are all fantastic at what you do. You all populate this book. But, a special shout out to Michael, and the memories that keep Phil and Kevin in our hearts.

To the producers who brought shows into our houses and treated the staff like family: thanks.

At the office: Peter, Mary

It's been an incredible, unprecedented experience working on Broadway. I'd never have thought this life could or would exist.

Lastly, I thank everyone at Sound Associates for giving me a new lease on my Broadway life in 2021 and beyond.

Curtain Up!

**JOSEPH PITTMAN** is a veteran of Broadway, having worked Front of House for more than 30 years. As an usher and ticket taker and sound associate, he helps ensure theater patrons have a memorable experience at their show.

He is also the author of over 40 books, including the acclaimed "Linden Corners" novels—TILTING AT WINDMILLS, A CHRISTMAS WISH, A CHRISTMAS HOPE, A CHRISTMAS DREAM, and CHASING WINDMILLS. As a mystery novelist, his Todd Gleason series features LONDON FROG, CALIFORNIA SCHEMING, TWO TODD TALES, TWO MORE TODD TALES, and THE CANNES CON.

Under the pseudonym ADAM CARPENTER, he is best known for the best-selling "Jimmy McSwain Files," featuring a gay private detective in Hell's Kitchen, and whose mother is the head usher at a Broadway Theatre. Those books include HIDDEN IDENTITY, CRIME WAVE, STAGE FRIGHT, GUARDIAN ANGEL, FOREVER HAUNT, FRESH KILL, and SECOND SHOT.

He has also written a book with his dog, Shadow, called THE SHADOW DIARIES. He lives in New Jersey with husband, Steve, but still calls Broadway home.

For more information, visit lindencornerspress.com.

www.ingramcontent.com/pod-product-compliance
Lightning Source LLC
Chambersburg PA
CBHW070501120526
44590CB00013B/715